THE NEW HOMEOWNER'S HANDBOOK

WHAT TO DO AFTER YOU MOVE IN

Nehemiah Corporation with
Barbara B. Buchholz and Margaret Crane

DEARBORN™

A **Kaplan Professional** Company

This publication is designed to provide accurate and authoritative information in regard to the subject matter covered. It is sold with the understanding that the publisher is not engaged in rendering legal, accounting, or other professional service. If legal advice or other expert assistance is required, the services of a competent professional should be sought.

Acquisitions Editor: Mary B. Good
Senior Managing Editor: Jack Kiburz
Interior Design: Lucy Jenkins
Cover Design: Salvatore Concialdi
Typesetting: the dotted i

Published by Dearborn, a Kaplan Professional Company

Printed in the United States of America

00 01 02   10 9 8 7 6 5 4 3 2 1

Library of Congress Cataloging-in-Publication Data
The new homeowner's handbook : what to do after you move in / Nehemiah Corporation with Barbara B. Buchholz & Margaret Crane.
    p.   cm.
    Includes bibliographical references and index.
    ISBN 0-7931-3818-3 (paper)
    1. Home ownership—United States.   I. Buchholz, Barbara Ballinger.
II. Crane, Margaret.   III. Nehemiah Corporation.
HD7287.82.U484   2000
643'.12—dc21
                                     00-020415

Dedication

To our families and all families who have held
on to their share of the American dream.

CONTENTS

FOREWORD

There is a place where people find courage and joy; a place where children find security and support; a place where memories are created, values are practiced, and families come together. This place is called home.

Nehemiah Corporation, a charitable housing organization, was formed in 1994. In 1997, we established The Nehemiah Program, the largest privately funded down payment assistance program in the nation. If Mom and Dad can't help, we can. Nehemiah Corporation is dedicated to increasing home ownership opportunities and the success of homeowners.

We realize that a home is a sacred place to be nurtured, embraced, and respected. Housing is not a luxury but a fundamental need that furthers the social well-being of individuals, families, and the economy.

Home ownership not only represents a major purchase but also a lifelong commitment—a commitment to family and neighborhood and an investment in communities across the country. It represents the reward of hard work, dedication, stability, and pride.

In continuing our mission of increasing home ownership opportunities and homeowner success, we have produced *The New Homeowner's Handbook: What to Do After You Move In* as part of our commitment to homeowners who are discovering the joys of owning a home and the challenges they may face. This book embodies our philosophy of helping people to help themselves and will provide homeowners with useful information to help them make informed decisions. *The New Homeowner's Handbook* is designed to ensure that home ownership becomes everything they have dreamed.

Nehemiah Corporation wishes you success and joy in your achievement of the American dream. For further information related to this book or Nehemiah Corporation, please call 800-853-1937 or visit our Web site at <www.nehemiahprogram.org>.

ACKNOWLEDGMENTS

Many experts contributed directly and indirectly to this book.

Without the unstinting encouragement and sharp red pencil of Mary B. Good, acquisitions editor at Dearborn in Chicago, this book would not have been possible and would not be as thorough as it is.

A number of people offered help and practical suggestions at various stages of our research and writing. Their candid comments helped make the process a pleasure and an adventure, and improved the final product. We have attempted to list all who assisted us; if we have left out anyone, please forgive us and know we greatly appreciated your help.

Our thanks go to Kenneth T. Austin, president of House-Master, a home inspection franchise company, located in Bound Brook, New Jersey, and operating throughout the United States and Canada. Kenneth contributed enormously with his sense of humor and helpful suggestions. We are deeply grateful for advice and comments from the people at Beckmann Brothers Inc., a garden store in St. Louis; to Sean Closkey, executive director of the St. Joseph's Carpenter Society, a nonprofit housing developer in Camden, New Jersey; to Steven H. Domsky, a registered representative with Mass Mutual in Chicago; to Mary Salinis Duron, first vice president and director of fair lending, and Virginia Martinez, vice president for city development, both of Countrywide HomeAmerica Loans, headquartered in Calabasas, California; to Brooke Givot of First Impressions in Chicago, an interior designer who helps to decorate homes and prepare them for resale; to St. Louis attorneys Sheldon Grand and T.J. Mullin; to Simon Hakin, professor of economics, affiliated with the *Privatization* Research Center at Temple University in Philadelphia; to Laura L. Herring, president and CEO of The IMPACT Group in St. Louis; to Lt. David Hodges of the Ladue, Missouri, police force; to David Lowell, education manager for the Associated Locksmiths of America in Dallas; to Rob Matheny of Matheny Heating and Cooling in St. Louis; to Joel Rey-Barreau, consulting director of education for the Lighting and Design Center of the University of Kentucky in Lexington; to Cindy Riordan of the Neighborhood Stabilization Team of the City of St. Louis; to Eric Shanks, personal lines manager of the St. Louis office of Chubb Group of Insurance Cos. (based in Warren, N.J.); to Schnarr True Value Hardware in St. Louis and to Brad Wastler, senior vice president of First National Bank of St. Louis.

We received additional help and comments from the people at American Lighting Association in Dallas; the National Association of Insurance Commissioners in Kansas City, Missouri; the National Burglar and Fire Alarm Association in Bethesda, Maryland; the National Crime Prevention Council in Washington, D.C.; the National Fire Protection Association in Quincy, Massachusetts; and the American Red Cross St. Louis Bi-State Chapter. Thanks also go to the people at several lawn and garden equipment stores in St. Louis: Milbradt, Art's Lawnmower, and Outdoor Equipment.

Finally, we thank those homeowners and individuals who shared their stories and insights. We hope that the how-to information in this book will help inspire those who either own their first home or plan to buy their first home in the near future. We wish them success and peace in their homes and throughout their lives.

Your New Home
Capturing and Keeping the American Dream

At last, you've found a wonderful home. Purchasing it is the fulfillment of the classic American dream: a house, a yard, and a car parked in the driveway or the garage. You felt the crackle of hope in the air when your bid was accepted and you staked your claim. The house represents the good life; it means happiness, security, and permanence.

But if you're not careful, the excitement of owning your own home can wear off faster than the thrill of a first love. Ownership represents hard work and a great deal of responsibility.

After all, a home is really just a bundle of bricks and plaster, paint, pipes, wires, floorboards, and walls. It can become a liability unless you're prepared financially, emotionally, and mentally for the many chores that lie ahead. If you're used to renting, the responsibility of owning a home can hit you like a ton of bricks. The reason? A home is a living commodity that constantly ages. It requires maintenance and upkeep. As it changes, it needs work, money, and other resources to keep it going. Any number of things can go wrong: your heater conks out, your wires need replacing and updating, the toilet overflows, water pipes burst—maybe in the middle of the night—or horror of horrors, termites turn up in the crawl space.

Emergency repairs can throw you a big financial curveball. When you rented, you became upset when problems occurred, but there was a significant difference. You called your building's manager or superintendent to come and make repairs or find someone who could. No longer do you have that luxury when your dwelling belongs to you. Now there's no one on call to fix any problems except your favorite handy uncle or the repair person whose services you really can't afford this month. And if something needs to be replaced, it can be even more expensive.

It is likely that you have bought an old house, and you may not be used to the problems that arise with a dated home. You may encounter lead-based paint, asbestos, radon and other gas leaks, worn insulation or no insulation, frayed wiring or insufficient electrical power. Are the roof and all its shingles still intact? Are there smoke alarms and do they work? What about the plumbing? These aren't very attractive items to spend your hard-earned dollars on when you would rather enjoy new furniture. If you're pressed for funds, you may be tempted to put maintenance charges on your credit card and worry about paying them off later.

And remember, you also need to spend money on annual repairs and ongoing maintenance, taxes, utilities, and insurance premiums. And you still have all of your day-to-day living expenses—food, clothing, medical care, occasional entertainment, and so on.

You can beat any problem if you're motivated. When ownership goes awry, it is usually due to the lack of money to do what the owner wants and needs to do. But the good news is that money can be stretched. There are ways to cut your bills and secrets to help you save more and invest profitably. With this book you will learn how to:

- Pay off credit card debt.
- Use free home decorating advice to beautify your home.
- Fight city hall to lower property taxes.

- Shop for cheaper insurance.
- Reduce energy and repair costs.
- Budget and invest wisely while paying off your home.
- Save money for emergencies.
- Slash your mortgage if interest rates change.
- Make money from your old stuff.

Here's a real-life example of how one couple fared. Jane and Adam Johnson (not their real names) are typical first-time homeowners. They were in a rush to buy their new home, eager to start putting down permanent roots. They had always rented but were tired of throwing their rent money away, particularly once their third child arrived. Their two-bedroom apartment was bursting at the seams. Although they comfortably afforded their monthly rent, they didn't have extra money socked away for a down payment.

Eventually, the Johnsons found a home in a nice neighborhood with good schools nearby. When a mortgage broker pointed out that interest rates had fallen quite low, they decided they would not wait any longer. The Johnsons shifted into high gear. They gathered enough money to make a 10 percent down payment, and they were able to get a mortgage for the remaining 90 percent. They felt that with their combined monthly salaries they could comfortably handle the mortgage, which included property taxes and insurance.

The Johnsons soon discovered that the mortgage was the tip of the expense iceberg. As homeowners, they now had to take on all the responsibilities of being in charge of their own property. As they shifted from a renter's to a homeowner's mentality, they found the transition difficult. A wise developer once remarked, "There's a metaphysical desire for us to own our own homes, but if anything goes wrong, the first-time homeowner wants someone else to be the owner and take care of the problems." The Johnsons quickly realized that they needed a house plan in the same way that a business owner needs a business plan.

Like the Johnsons, you, too, may have rented most of your life. When you become a homeowner, you may be surprised when you are suddenly bombarded with changes and charges. Learning how to become a smart, prudent homeowner is like learning how to parent. In both cases, there are definite lessons to learn and guidelines to follow. Your home will be as good to you, providing safe and comfortable shelter, as long as you are good to it. The old cliche—you get out of it what you put into it—is never more true than when it comes to home ownership.

This book reinforces that truism. It is arranged in six chapters that you can easily consult when you need information on insurance, safety and security, neighborliness, financial planning, inexpensive decorating, and repairs and maintenance.

There are many sources of information in addition to books like this one. Nonprofit lending agencies, affordable-housing developers, and credit counselors offer numerous resources such as classes, advice, and information on repairs and maintenance, financial planning, decorating, safety, credit, insurance, and other topics. The Internet offers a host of free information on home ownership on countless Web sites. Home improvement and decorating centers organize regular home ownership classes too. Videos and TV shows demonstrate hands-on advice for repairing and maintaining items in your home. Community colleges arrange classes for homeowning do-it-yourselfers and others who want information for a nominal price.

You will quickly learn that there are pros and cons to home ownership. On the good side, a house is yours for as long as you make monthly payments, including insurance and taxes, and as long as you keep up the maintenance. So you have to plan and budget to build up the equity in your home, which is the portion of the principal that has been paid off. As your home increases in value, the value of your equity rises, too. As a homeowner you also enjoy tax benefits. Interest payments and property tax payments are deductible, and if you moved into the house because of a job relocation, the cost of the move may be deductible as well. Your home is a very smart investment.

Now for the drawbacks. You have less mobility when you own your home rather than rent because you can't just pick up and leave when the lease is up. You have to sell your home, and in many areas a home must really be up to snuff before it is even put on the market for resale. Furthermore, costs in your home don't remain the same; they tend to go up and up. Even if you have a 30-year fixed mortgage, your payments can rise as property taxes increase or insurance rates inch up. (Later we'll address what to do in these cases and how you can avoid some of the costs.) Most important, you must not miss mortgage payments and end up defaulting on your mortgage. If you do, you may lose your home and whatever you've invested in it.

You must not allow yourself to be seduced into borrowing for improvements, even if you want to change the tile in your bathroom or purchase that living room furniture you've been dying to own. Once you're a homeowner, solicitations come over the phone and through the mail faster than a hurricane. It seems that everybody wants to lend you money or extend your line of credit. "It's so simple," they say. "Just sign on the dotted line. Take out a short-term loan from a credit or loan company, or take a cash advance on your credit card. You can afford these improvements." You might take these salespeople up on their offers, especially when an emergency arises. But if you do, you may find you've dug yourself deeper into debt, into a financial hole that you can't get out of.

To avoid a debt trap, you need a plan. And just like players in any game, you must shift your position from time to time. Changing spending habits is difficult and requires a complete overhaul of your lifestyle and mind-set, but it may be necessary in order for you to achieve homeowning success.

Even in the worst-case scenarios, all is not hopeless, but you must create a plan to regain control. All the education in the world will not help if you do not stick to certain rules. Budgeting is like a diet. If you lose pounds on a temporary basis then resume your previous fattening eating patterns and sedentary lifestyle, you will fail.

Owning your own home is a chance to test yourself, to work harder, to be better prepared, and to focus on taking care of your surroundings. Yes, there will be problems along the way, but there also will be great joy and satisfaction for your entire family. You need to view the passage to home ownership as a wonderful challenge now and far into the future. If you stay informed, refuse to procrastinate, and are determined to learn from your mistakes, you will be undertaking one of the most satisfying journeys of your life. Knowledge, you will find, will become your most important asset when it comes to keeping and enjoying your home.

1

Insurance

Protecting Your Property and Valuables

After you've worked hard to buy your house, you're probably eager to spend any leftover funds to decorate or remodel, or to begin saving for the future. The last thing you probably want to do right now is to spend money on something you can't touch or get your arms around, but you must. You need to buy homeowners insurance to protect your dream. In fact, mortgage companies require it because they must protect their investment. You should also consider buying liability, life, and disability insurance to ensure that you will always be able to pay your premiums.

Homeowners Insurance

What's the probability that an emergency will occur? Unfortunately, it's fairly high. An old wire can cause a fire that will quickly destroy part or all of your house, or a flood can send water flowing through your basement and even—in a worst-case scenario—uproot your house along with stately old trees and luscious green sod.

Even if you're fortunate and nothing terrible happens, minor mishaps routinely occur that seem pretty terrible at the time. Your television or VCR may be stolen, particularly if you don't have a burglar alarm system or occasionally forget to lock your doors. A faulty air conditioner may send water overflowing from a pan into your living or sleeping quarters. Then that lovely paint you just applied will need to be freshened.

You buy homeowners insurance to gain protection for your house and its contents in case a loss occurs that you can't pay for out of pocket.

When you buy homeowners insurance, you must make numerous decisions. You must choose the right type of policy (or policies), and the right amount of coverage.

The task can be difficult because there are no cookie-cutter recommendations for every homeowner to follow. The type and amount of homeowners insurance that is right for you and your vintage clapboard home in the city may be quite different from coverage your cousin needs for her brick house in the suburbs and her large collection of antiques. And both may differ from coverage your uncle bought to protect his A-frame vacation home on the hurricane-prone North Carolina shore. The location of a dwelling, its size, construction, and age, and your prior loss history all factor into the insurance coverage equation.

What It Costs and What's Covered

Before you finalize your decision, you should familiarize yourself with the terms you're likely to encounter in the lengthy insurance policy document: replaceable cost or replacement value coverage, actual cash or market value, depreciation, rider and floater, subrogation—the list goes on and on. Once you get comfortable with those terms, you're ready to weigh the different pricetags for the coverage you'll consider. Few policies can be compared, however, in the same way that you would compare one 24-ounce bottle of bleach to another of a different brand. It's not so cut-and-dried. You have to take into account numerous factors:

- How much is the premium—the price you pay for the policy?
- What does the policy cover—your house, your detached garage (referred to as an appurtenant structure), a treehouse, your landscaping, your valuables, or only some of those?
- How much is the deductible—the money you pay if you file a claim? (No company covers everything 100 percent.)
- How long does the policy last? (Limited duration policies may be tempting, but they are relatively costly.)
- What does the policy exclude (like damage from a windstorm or flooding)?
- How difficult is it to cancel the policy once you have purchased it?

Any detached structures will be protected by your policy but not to the same extent as your main dwelling. The value of a detached unit is usually limited to between 10 and 20 percent of the total value of your home, so the garage of a $150,000 home usually won't be covered for more than $15,000 to $30,000. You can increase the amount covered if your garage houses your toy soldier collection, but you'll need to weigh the extra cost versus the collection's value. You're probably realizing very quickly how important mathematics is, so grab your calculator before you start figuring various options.

Your landscaping is another separate entity that is covered by your homeowners policy, but typically for only 5 percent of the value of your home and with certain upper limits. Chubb, a personal and commercial property consulting and liability company, for example, does not cover any single tree, shrub, or plant for more than $1,000, even if you shipped it in from an expensive nursery. Furthermore, few policies cover your lawn, shrubs, and trees against every disaster. Fire, lightning, and explosions are covered; windstorms may not be.

When it comes to the deductible, typically you have to pay the first $250 or $500 on your own before your company's coverage kicks in. The lower the deductible the higher the premium and vice versa.

Insurance coverage usually must be adjusted periodically because most houses and their contents increase in value and people's life situations change. Children are born, and possessions multiply; children marry and move away, and fewer possessions are needed. When a third child is born, you may build an addition to your home, necessitating an increase in coverage.

Riders

You may also want to buy a rider or personal articles floater to cover your expensive personal items such as jewelry, furs, and artworks, because most homeowners' policies set a general limit of $2,000 per item. (If you pay to raise that limit, this is known as an endorsement.) Riders can vary tremendously in the amounts they cover, so it's wise to check the fine print carefully. A typical policy may limit coverage on silverware to $1,000 to $5,000 no matter how many cutlery pieces you have or how valuable they are, and business equipment such as computers and fax machines may be limited to $1,000 to $10,000, even if you have an elaborate home office and have several people working in your home with you.

A rider requires you to separately "schedule," or list, your valuables by having them appraised. Generally, riders are not subject to a deductible, and they cover items wherever they are, with certain stipulations. If you leave the country with the insured items, for example, certain companies will set a limit. Riders can be expensive, but they can be well worth the cost.

Replacement Cost versus Actual Cash Value Policies

Once you understand the basics of homeowners insurance, you're ready to make your first critical decision: Should you cover your house with a replacement cost or actual cash value policy? Replacement cost coverage is more expensive but also more comprehensive. If your house is completely destroyed, for example, the insurance company will pay you the amount of money that will be needed to replace the house and its contents. If your furniture was worn, that doesn't matter. You will receive the amount of money needed to buy a new living room set to replace the old one.

Generally, especially in cities, the replacement cost of a house is substantially higher than its market value (what you could sell the house for), so some owners choose not to pay the higher premiums necessary to insure their home 100 percent. Even if you reason that your house will never be totally destroyed, you still should insure it at 100 percent of replacement cost to protect yourself. The mortgage companies require it anyway in most cases.

If you are the type of person who always wants to be on the safe side, you may want to invest in guaranteed replacement cost coverage, which is a promise on the insurance company's part to rebuild your home or restore it to its prior condition regardless of the cost. Payment on policies without this guarantee stops at the policy limit.

The lot on which your house rests is a different matter, regardless of what type of replacement policy you choose. The insurance company usually will pay for you to rebuild on the same site, giving you nothing for the lot itself, because it's assumed the land withstood the disaster. Therefore, you won't be able to take your insurance money and build in Boulder, Colorado, if your current location is in Chicago, Illinois. A few companies, however, do offer a relocation option, so ask in advance.

The other choice—actual cash value coverage—is less costly than replacement value coverage, but it has a downside. Actual cash value coverage takes into account depreciation—the fact that you've lived in and "used" your house and any contents so that they're technically not worth as much as they once were. For example, if a tornado destroys the bed that cost you $600 five years ago, a replacement cost policy will pay the $800 it now costs to buy a new one. An actual cash value policy, on the other hand, will give you maybe $300 because the bed's lifespan is halfway finished and the bed isn't worth as much as it once was.

A decided advantage of an actual cash value policy is that you don't have to rebuild on the same site. You can take the funds you receive and build anywhere in the world, from Boulder, Colorado, to Santa Monica, California.

Whichever you choose, you may want to be sure your policy has an inflation guard clause that increases coverage periodically according to specific formula in order to keep pace with inflation.

Which Perils Do You Want Covered, Both Inside and Out?

Besides the question of replacement cost or actual cash value, you have several other important decisions to make, including what types of peril you want your house protected against. The more perils you cite, the greater the cost. There are six basic homeowner policies, all identified by the letters "HO" for homeowner, plus a number. Most homeowners, however, are unaware that all these types of coverage are available.

The most basic policy, designated HO-1, covers against losses from 11 types of peril: fire or lightning, windstorm or hail, explosion, riot or civil commotion, aircraft, vehicles, smoke, vandalism or malicious mischief, theft, damage by glass or safety glazing, and volcanic eruptions.

An HO-2 policy adds six more perils to the list: falling objects, including trees; weight of ice, snow, or sleet; electrical surge damages; and water-related damage from three sources or causes: home utilities or appliances, sonic booms, and frozen pipes.

HO-3 policies are very popular because they include coverage for all risks and perils except those listed as exclusions; an HO-5 is similar, but it covers more risks and perils than does an HO-3.

HO-4 policies are for renters.

HO-6 policies are for owners who live in multiunit buildings such as a condominiums or cooperative buildings. These policies can insure interior walls, fixtures, appliances, and personal property. If you require an HO-6 policy, you should find out what your building association's insurance covers so you don't buy too much or too little coverage.

In addition to protecting your house, your homeowners insurance protects the objects within it, from basic odds and ends to family heirlooms of jewels and antiques. In most policies, this personal property coverage equals 50 to 70 percent of the value of your house. For a $150,000 house, then, belongings would be insured for between $75,000 and $105,000. You can indicate whether you want replacement cost or actual cash value coverage for your personal items, and you can buy additional coverage if you need it.

Policies also cover "loss of use," which means that if your home is destroyed or becomes uninhabitable, you will receive money that allows you to rent another home or stay in a hotel and eat out while your abode is rebuilt or remodeled. It's not necessarily as good as it sounds. It typically covers only a set time frame of about a year, and it is usually worth only 20 percent or so of the value of your home. With most companies, you can't stay in that fancy hotel forever.

Your policy should protect not just your home and its contents, but also your personal property offsite, typically at 10 percent of the contents' coverage. This comes in handy when you're on vacation or when your children go off to college.

While you're learning what your policy can cover, it's also important to understand that standard policies exclude damages occuring as a result of certain circumstances, like intentional acts such as the owner driving a car into the side of the house, or contamination due to pollution or smog.

Choosing the Company and/or Agent

Once you know what kind of coverage you want, you'll need to choose the company or individual from whom you'll purchase it. You have two major choices. You can buy homeowners insurance from a direct underwriter, specifically an agent who is an employee of a company such as Allstate or State Farm. Or you can go to an independent agency whose brokers represent several insurance companies.

Which is better? Not surprisingly, the independent agent route may be better because you get more consultation for your money. "The agent represents you in partnership with the company. He or she will also have a greater variety of products available for the owner while the direct writer usually has just one product to sell," explains Eric Shanks, personal lines manager for Chubb Group of Insurance Companies in St. Louis, Missouri. Others think independent agents are better because they work for more than one insurer and really represent you as you comparison shop. On the other hand, you may prefer to buy from a direct writer at a company whose name you know well.

In addition, check the number of complaints against the company, especially complaints for not paying claims. You can call your local better business bureau for a report, or check *Consumer Reports* in the reference department of your local library.

Because your agent is your regular contact for questions or problems, take care to select the right one. Look for a combination of experience and availability, and be sure that you and the agent have a good rapport. You want someone who is thorough, who dots all the i's and crosses all the t's on your coverage, but you also want someone you'll get along with, particularly in the event of a major disaster. If a fire has roared through your home, you will want someone with whom you feel comfortable to lead you through the long process of cleaning and replacing belongings and getting your home back to normal. You will have myriad questions and must be able to reach your agent easily.

Ask friends, relatives, and colleagues to recommend good agents. Be sure that the agent has the right credentials: CLU (Chartered Life Underwriter) or CPCU (Chartered Property Casualty Underwriter). Interview a few prospects and take into account your gut instincts; they're worth something.

There are a few questions you should ask an agent: How long have you been in business? What percentage of your claims get paid? Can I have the names and phone numbers of three clients as references? How many companies do you represent? Do you specialize in homeowners insurance?

You should also ask about the history and health of the company that issues the insurance. You want to be sure it will still be in business when you need it to pay out a claim. Check on a company's health by asking a ratings company for a report, for which you may have to pay a small fee. A few ratings companies to choose from are:

A. M. Best Company
Ambest Rd.
Oldwick, NJ 08858
908-439-2200
<www.ambest.com>

Duff & Phelps
55 E. Monroe St., Suite 3500
Chicago, IL 60603
312-368-3100
<www.dcrco.com>

Moody's Investors Service
Mergent Financial Information Services
60 Madison Ave., 6th Floor
New York, NY 10010
212-413-7601
<www.fisonline.com>

Standard & Poor's Corporation
55 Water St.
New York, NY 10041
212-438-2000
<www.standardandpoors.com/ratings>

Deciding How Much Coverage to Buy

The amount of coverage that is adequate for your home depends on a combination of factors, including the recent appraised value of your house and its contents. Your premium will be affected by where you live and the level of risk your home and its contents presents to your carrier. Most policies also set limits on coverage.

If your house is newer, it should be less likely than an older home to incur structural problems. Your home's susceptibility to burglary will depend in part on the community you live in. A burglar alarm can reduce the threat of a break in and help you to lower your coverage costs, sometimes by 10 to 15 percent.

Insurance companies limit coverage for money, coins, bank notes, and so on in order to encourage homeowners to insure such valuables separately. Coverage for them is limited to $100 under most policies, so it's risky to keep a large quantity of cash in the house. Also be aware that most policies set other limits such as $500 on a boat stored for the winter in your driveway. Of course, if you pay more, you can increase coverage for certain items.

Living in an area that is prone to natural disasters such as floods, earthquakes, or tornadoes may send your premium climbing. You might even have to buy additional coverage that may be expensive and have high deductibles. Earthquake coverage usually requires an extra policy and three separate deductibles of 5 to 15 percent of the loss amount. Because companies handle earthquake coverage in many different ways, you should be sure to ask about it if you live in an earthquake-prone area.

Flood insurance is available in participating communities through the National Flood Insurance Program, administered by the Federal Emergency Management Agency (FEMA). Call 800-638-6620 to find out if your community participates in the program. Ask what's covered and what's not. Fences and pools are not covered, for example.

Seven states provide special insurance plans to cover hurricane damage: Alabama, Florida, Louisiana, Mississippi, North Carolina, South Carolina, and Texas. Contact your state's underwriting association for more information.

If you live in a high-crime neighborhood, it may be difficult to buy a policy with standard coverage against theft and damage related to burglary. The Federal Crime Insurance Program may provide you with protection if you put in certain types of locks and other security devices.

Liability Insurance

A typical homeowners policy does more than protect your house and its contents. It also covers your legal liability if someone is injured on your property; for example, if someone slips on your icy driveway because you forgot to plow and sand it. Good personal liability coverage will pay not only for her surgery and recuperation but also for you to hire a lawyer when she sues you for negligence. Liability coverage also protects your credit cards if they're stolen when you're away on vacation. Of course, as with other types of coverage, there is a limit to the amount that can be recovered.

An umbrella policy, also known as personal excess insurance or a personal catastrophes policy, offers even more sweeping coverage. It's a separate policy that you purchase independently from your homeowners policy, but typically through the same carrier so that you'll receive a discount.

There are two ways that this type of policy can work. A "true" umbrella policy will cover everything on a primary basis up to a policy limit. So, if you have $300,000 in primary liability coverage and you purchase a $1 million umbrella policy, the umbrella covers any losses exceeding $300,000, up to the $1 million limit. An "excess" policy, on the other hand, would offer total coverage of $1.3 million because it stacks the two policies together.

Your Insurance Payment Plan

Because the cost of homeowners insurance is far from cheap, most companies do not insist that you pay the total amount up front. You can usually make monthly, quarterly, or biannual payments called premiums, though they usually will cost you a bit more than if you paid all at once. Your insurance and inter-

est payments can be folded into your regularly scheduled mortgage payment.

Taking Inventory of Your Possessions

If and when you need to file a claim, you will quickly discover the value of having completed a thorough home inventory: you will know right away what has been destroyed or
damaged or what is missing.

You can accomplish the inventory in several ways. You can
go through your home room by room and write a list by hand,
and if you have a computer you can transfer that data to a disk
and back it up for permanent safekeeping. You can record all of
the contents on video, naming them aloud as you go. Or you can
take pictures of everything then carefully label the photographs.
The Home Inventory Checklist on page 21 will help you to include everything.

Whichever method you choose, you should give a detailed
description of all your valuables, including specifics about their
dimensions, color, identifying marks, age, and both original and
current price. To substantiate your case if you should need to file
a claim, always save original receipts and provenances, which
provide the ownership history of valuable objects. Whenever
you make a large purchase, save the receipt and be sure it includes the store name, date purchased, and any serial numbers
or other identifying numbers.

For best results, you should go a step further and have a
professional appraiser provide the current valuation of anything
that's particularly valuable such as jewelry, artwork, furniture,
and collectibles. You can find appraisers in your area by looking
in the Yellow Pages or by calling one of two organizations: The
American Society of Appraisers in Washington, D.C., at 703-478-
2228, or the Appraisers Association of America in New York City
at 212-889-5404. Appraisers may charge for their services by the
hour or by the project, but rarely according to a percentage of the
value of the appraised items. The cost of hiring an appraiser may
be more than worthwhile if you have to file a claim.

To protect the records, store them somewhere safe, preferably away from your residence. The best places are in a safe-deposit box or at your lawyer's office; after all, if your house is destroyed your records will be as well.

Filing a Claim

If you have a claim to file, first notify the police, if necessary, then contact your agent. Take notes of your conversations. You may want to summarize them in a formal letter later. Save any receipts from temporary repairs, and expect a visit from an insurance adjuster if your claim is large—above $10,000 or $15,000.

You'll want to be careful about filing too many "minor" claims because the insurance company may or may not pay on them, and you also might send up a red flag, causing the company to increase your premiums when you go to renew. What's considered minor? It varies by company, but a minor loss might be anything under $1,000. Companies also look at the types of losses. One agent explains that maintenance losses such as a small tree falling and doing a bit of damage to a gutter, or coffee spilling onto a rug and ruining it, will cause more concern than a major fire loss. Furthermore, too many claims in a short period of time will also be carefully scrutinized. Making the call about when to file a claim is tough and a bit of a gamble, so sometimes it's wise to consult your agent for advice.

Business Liability and Mortgage Insurance

You may want some other specific types of insurance before you're through. Many people who work from home purchase business insurance to cover their business property and products and to protect themselves and their contacts from business liability.

Mortgage insurance can ensure that your mortgage will be paid off if you die or become disabled. In many cases it's required by your mortgage lender. Check with your real estate agent or mortgage broker.

Life Insurance

You probably think your homeowners insurance coverage is sufficient to protect the investment you have made in your house. That may be so in a best-case scenario, or if you have no dependents. Often, however, homeowners insurance is insufficient. Many families need something more, such as life insurance, to be able to continue paying the bills (including other insurance premiums) if the main breadwinner in the family dies.

Imagine this: The main income-producing member of your household dies suddenly, and you, the survivor, do not work at all, work part-time, or have been out of the workforce for a while so you don't have the skills to get a job with high enough pay. Furthermore, you have several young children, and they are not old enough to help earn income to put bread on the table.

You wonder and you worry. How will you and your dependents continue to stay in your home, pay the mortgage, buy groceries, and pay for all the expenses you incur day in and day out? Life insurance can make all the difference in the world, particularly because life insurance payouts are not subject to federal and state taxes.

To decide how much life insurance to buy for your family, you need to analyze your typical monthly and annual expenses. You should buy enough insurance, but you don't want to buy too much because the premium takes money away from other necessary expenditures. Once you know your total expenses, you need to figure out what monies you will have available from Social Security survivor benefits, savings, and any real estate. You may find that you will have sufficient funds to get by for a few months or even longer, but you will need to think about what you will do after that time has passed.

Your family may be like numerous others that find themselves seriously cash strapped and need to quickly fill in the gap—which is more like a chasm in some cases. How much is enough? Insurance experts like Steven H. Domsky, a registered representative with Mass Mutual in Chicago, generally recommend that a family with two children should buy life insurance equal to 8 to 12 times the parents' combined annual gross income.

After you have a total amount of insurance in mind, you need to decide what type to buy: term or cash value (also known as whole life). Domsky compares term insurance to monthly rental costs for a house or apartment. The costs will go up as time goes by and eventually the insurance company will terminate your policy, possibly when you are age 80 or so. He adds that many holders terminate the term policies earlier as the costs become prohibitive and once their children are grown and out of college.

You can regularly renew a term policy at intervals of 5, 10, 20, or 30 years. Most quality companies do not require you to submit to a medical exam each time you extend your policy, though the rates will go up after the specified lock-in period is completed. Also, premiums will increase as you get older because you face a greater chance of dying. When you die, your beneficiaries will receive proceeds from the policy equal to the amount of the net death benefit, also referred to as the face amount of the policy.

Let's take a hypothetical case. If you make $30,000 a year, you would be wise to purchase a $250,000 term policy. If you are a male in very good health, such a policy would probably cost $170 a year. Upon your death, your beneficiary would inherit $250,000, tax free.

In contrast, whole life insurance provides lifetime coverage, and it also features a savings component. Those savings gradually build up. For the same $250,000 of coverage, a whole life policy would cost a much steeper $2,180 a year. But when the insured dies, let's say at age 60 of prostate cancer, the total benefits will have grown to a whopping $460,000. The value buildup is tax deferred, and the death benefit is usually tax free for the beneficiary. Therefore, a whole life policy may be a good investment for your heirs.

There are many variations of both types of policies. For example, a variable life policy allows the insured to link the premium to a separate account, so the funds are comparable to a 401(k). The bottom-line advantage of a variable life policy is that it allows the premium to be invested in an equity-like product rather than in the bond market as whole life premiums are.

The tricky part is asking all the essential questions before you put down money for a life insurance policy. One man asks another in a radio insurance ad, "Which would you rather do, talk to an insurance expert about the type of life insurance to buy, or have root canal?" The response: "I'd rather have root canal." Sorting through the life insurance maze can indeed be challenging, especially if you don't have a good sense of direction.

Before you buy, first find out how long the company has been in business and what its financial stability is like. You want to know what the guarantees of the policy are. There are almost 2,000 life insurance companies operating in the U.S., Domsky says, and the premiums they offer vary greatly. Your agent should be able to supply you with information on insurance company ratings. You also should ask whether the policy pays dividends, whether it's automatically renewable, whether it offers loan rights and can be used to help pay a mortgage, whether it includes a grace period and how long that period lasts, how long it takes for the insurance carrier to pay on a claim, what circumstances, like suicide, an airplane crash, or overly dangerous activities, like hang gliding, will disallow payment, and whether there are any stipulations regarding the naming of beneficiaries.

Disability Insurance

You would be wise to look into buying disability insurance as well as life insurance. This can help you pay bills if a breadwinner becomes disabled and is therefore temporarily or permanently unable to go back to work. In their book, *Winning the Insurance Game: The Complete Consumer's Guide to Saving Money*, Ralph Nader and Wesley J. Smith term disability insurance as "income replacement policy," and that is what it is—it replaces lost income for a set time frame or indefinitely.

Before you purchase disability insurance, you should evaluate what your employer offers in its group plan and decide if the coverage is sufficient. Domsky explains that most employer plans are insufficient. The reason? A typical policy covers only 60 percent of your base salary, and that 60 percent is fully taxable, leaving you with less than 50 percent of your current level of income.

That 50 percent may not be enough if you are young and your Social Security benefits haven't yet kicked in, and if you will not be receiving workers' compensation. If that is the case, you may want to add extra coverage through a private policy, the money from which would not be taxed.

How much disability insurance do you need? It depends on your income and expenses and whether there is a second wage earner. Many insurance experts suggest a premium amount equal to 1 to 2 percent of gross household income. A person who earns $40,000 might purchase a disability insurance policy that costs between $400 and $800 per year. This might seem steep, but it will be well worth the investment if something catastrophic happens.

Although it may seem tempting to buy even more disability insurance—as much as you can afford—you generally cannot buy coverage for more than 70 percent of your current gross income. The reason is pretty straightforward: Most insurance companies want to encourage you to return to work as soon as possible so they can stop making payments to you.

You also need to look at your savings to see if you would be able to wait for a while to collect, because many policies have a three- to six-month waiting period, called an "elimination period." The higher the deductible and the longer the elimination period, the less expensive the premium.

When comparing policies, check whether they state if you have to be unable to work in "your own occupation" or "any occupation." It may make a difference in how quickly you'll be expected to get back to your job. Also, look at what the policy states regarding full-time or part-time work. Go through a policy with an agent if you don't understand any terms, says Eric Shanks of Chubb Group of Insurance Companies.

Ask how long benefits will last—a year, a few years, or a lifetime. What situations are excluded and would prevent funds from being paid out? Disabilities resulting from attempted suicide, drug abuse, airplane crashes, service in the military, normal pregnancy, and mental illness are sometimes excluded. You also need to know if the policy can be canceled, and whether it is guaranteed or is only conditionally renewable. Ask whether benefits are adjusted for inflation and whether the level of your premium is guaranteed. Finally, most companies do not offer a discount if you purchase both life and disability insurance from them, so it is best to work with an agent who has the broadest knowledge of the products available in the marketplace.

There are two big mistakes that most people make concerning life and disability coverage. Most people don't buy enough life insurance, and most people don't buy any disability coverage, according to Domsky. A good resource to consult when making decisions about the quantity and type of insurance to buy is *Ernst & Young's Personal Financial Planning Guide*.

Finally, whatever insurance you decide to buy, be sure to review your coverage annually and make the necessary adjustments, just as you go for an annual physical checkup and make changes to improve your health. If your insurance is too low, you can always add more.

If You Are Refused Coverage

Are there any grounds for an insurance company to refuse coverage? Yes. For example, a company may refuse coverage if you want to insure your home for less than 80 percent of its value; if you have a bad prior loss history; or if certain characteristics of your home, like great distance from the nearest fire department, make it hard to protect.

Resources

Appraisal Institute
875 N. Michigan Ave., Suite 2400
Chicago, IL 60611
312-335-4100
<www.appraisalinstitute.org>

American Association of Retired
  Persons
601 E St., NW
Washington, DC 20049
800-424-3410
<www.aarp.org>

Consumer Federation of America
1424 16th St., NW, Suite 604
Washington, DC 20036
202-387-6121
<www.consumerfed.org>

Independent Insurance Agents of
  America
127 South Peyton St.
Alexandria, VA 22314
703-683-4422
<www.independentagent.com>

Insurance Information
  Institute
110 William St.
New York, NY 10038
800-331-9146
<www.iii.org>

National Association of
  Professional Insurance
  Agents
400 N. Washington St.
Alexandria, VA 22314
703-836-9340
<www.pianet.com>

National Insurance
  Consumer Help Line
800-942-4242

Additional Reading

- *Family Insurance Handbook: The Complete Guide for the 1990s,* by Les Abromovitz (Liberty Hall Press, 1990)
- *The Complete Book of Insurance: The Consumer's Guide to Insuring Your Life, Health, Property and Income,* by Ben G. Baldwin (Probus, 1996)
- *Total Coverage: The Complete Insurance and Security Guide,* by Darcie Bundy and Stuart Day (Perennial Library, 1987)
- *If You're Clueless about Insurance and Want to Know More,* by Seth Godin (Dearborn, 1998)

- *Winning the Insurance Game: The Complete Consumer's Guide to Saving Money,* by Ralph Nader and Wesley J. Smith (Doubleday, 1990)
- *How to Get Your Money's Worth in Home and Auto Insurance,* by Barbara Taylor (McGraw-Hill, 1991)

State Insurance Departments

Alabama 334-269-3550

Alaska 907-465-2515

Arizona 602-912-8400

Arkansas 501-371-2600

California 916-492-3500

Colorado 303-894-7499

Connecticut 860-297-3800

Delaware 302-739-4251

District of Columbia
202-727-8000

Florida 850-922-3130

Georgia 404-656-2056

Hawaii 808-586-2790

Idaho 208-334-4250

Illinois 217-785-0116

Indiana 317-232-2385

Iowa 515-281-5705

Kansas 785-296-7801

Kentucky 502-564-6027

Louisiana 504-868-1886

Maine 207-624-8475

Maryland 410-468-2090

Massachusetts 617-521-7794

Michigan 517-373-0220

Minnesota 651-296-6848

Mississippi 601-359-3569

Missouri 573-751-4126

Montana 406-444-2040

Nebraska 402-471-2201

Nevada 775-687-4270

New Hampshire 603-271-2261

New Jersey 609-292-5350

New Mexico 505-827-4601

New York 212-480-6400

North Carolina 919-733-7349

North Dakota 701-328-2440

Ohio 614-644-2658

Oklahoma 405-521-2686

Oregon 888-877-4894

Pennsylvania 717-783-0442

Puerto Rico 787-722-8686

Rhode Island 401-222-2223

South Carolina 803-737-6160

South Dakota 605-773-3563

Tennessee 615-741-2176

Texas 512-463-6464

Utah 801-538-3800

Vermont 802-828-3301

Virginia 804-371-9694

Virgin Islands 340-774-7166

Washington 360-753-7301

West Virginia 304-558-3354

Wisconsin 608-266-0102

Wyoming 307-777-7401

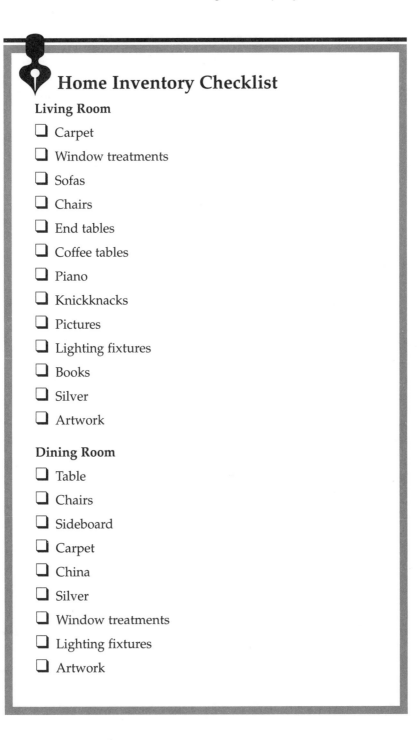

Home Inventory Checklist

Living Room

❑ Carpet

❑ Window treatments

❑ Sofas

❑ Chairs

❑ End tables

❑ Coffee tables

❑ Piano

❑ Knickknacks

❑ Pictures

❑ Lighting fixtures

❑ Books

❑ Silver

❑ Artwork

Dining Room

❑ Table

❑ Chairs

❑ Sideboard

❑ Carpet

❑ China

❑ Silver

❑ Window treatments

❑ Lighting fixtures

❑ Artwork

Home Inventory Checklist
(continued)

Kitchen

❑ Cabinets

❑ Large appliances

❑ Small appliances

❑ Lighting fixtures

❑ Window treatments

❑ Dishes

❑ Silverware

❑ Glassware

❑ Cookbooks

❑ Television

❑ Radio

❑ Artwork

Family Room or Den

❑ Carpet

❑ Lighting fixtures

❑ Window treatments

❑ Sofas

❑ Chairs

❑ Coffee tables

❑ End tables

❑ Books

❑ Television

❑ Radio

Home Inventory Checklist
(continued)

❑ Stereo

❑ Pictures

❑ Odds and ends

❑ Artwork

Bedroom 1

❑ Window treatments

❑ Carpet

❑ Lighting fixtures

❑ Bed

❑ End tables

❑ Chaise or chair

❑ Clothing

❑ Books

❑ Pictures

❑ Mirror

❑ Artwork

Bedroom 2

❑ Window treatments

❑ Carpet

❑ Lighting fixtures

❑ Bed

❑ End tables

❑ Chaise or chair

Home Inventory Checklist
(continued)

- ❏ Clothing
- ❏ Books
- ❏ Pictures
- ❏ Mirror
- ❏ Artwork

Bedroom 3
- ❏ Window treatments
- ❏ Carpet
- ❏ Lighting fixtures
- ❏ Bed
- ❏ End tables
- ❏ Chaise or chair
- ❏ Clothing
- ❏ Books
- ❏ Pictures
- ❏ Mirror
- ❏ Artwork

Bathroom 1
- ❏ Window treatments
- ❏ Cosmetics
- ❏ Jewelry
- ❏ Mirrors
- ❏ Linens

Home Inventory Checklist

(continued)

Bathroom 2

☐ Window treatments

☐ Cosmetics

☐ Jewelry

☐ Mirrors

☐ Linens

Bathroom 3

☐ Window treatments

☐ Cosmetics

☐ Jewelry

☐ Mirrors

☐ Linens

Basement

☐ Sofas

☐ Chairs

☐ Rug

☐ Books

☐ Television

☐ Radio

☐ Washer/Dryer

☐ Pool table

☐ Ping-pong table

☐ Ironing board

☐ Odds and ends

Home Inventory Checklist
(continued)

Attic or Storage Area

☐ Suitcases

☐ Clothing

☐ Books

☐ Baby clothing

☐ Pictures

☐ Memorabilia

Garage

☐ Lawnmower

☐ Snow blower

☐ Gardening equipment

☐ Bicycles

☐ Other sports equipment

☐ Garden furniture

2

Home Security and Safety from Natural Disasters

Preventing Burglary

You may or may not be old enough to remember the good old days when you could leave your house or your car unlocked. In many parts of the country, you still can be quite cavalier about safety. Unfortunately, however, in a growing number of cities, towns, suburbs, and rural areas you no longer can.

But don't panic. You don't have to turn your brand new home into a fortress or prison. In fact, burglaries nationwide have been declining rather than increasing, particularly in the urban areas that often have the worst crime statistics.

In 1997, the latest year for which statistics are available, burglaries had dropped 3 percent from the previous year, according to the National Burglar and Fire Alarm Association in Bethesda, Maryland.

But don't get cocky and start leaving your doors open. Even though the decline in crime bodes well, there is still a staggering number of burglaries being committed; according to the National Crime Prevention Council, one out of every ten homes is burglarized each year. A burglary occurs every few seconds, and one can be completed before you can finish asking, "Did I hear something odd or was it my imagination?"

When a burglary occurs, the costs quickly add up. Every year, more than $3.3 billion is lost nationwide in residential burglaries, with the average loss at a fairly significant $1,300. And those figures don't include all that is damaged in a forced entry. Windows and doors may be broken, locks may be mangled, and furniture or other items may be damaged.

According to one Midwestern suburban police lieutenant, residential burglaries occur most often in the early evening and decrease after 10 PM when it is assumed that people return home. They are also commonplace in the daytime because so many people work or leave their doors open. "Burglaries are crimes of opportunity," says Lieutenant D. Hodges of the Ladue, Missouri, police force. Many criminals are quite clever in following their potential victims' comings and goings and detecting a set pattern for when they go to work, walk the dog, or pick up children at school.

According to the FBI crime statistics for 1996, the last year for which figures are available, two out of every three burglaries are residential in nature; 66 percent involve forced entry, 26 percent unlawful entry without force; 51 percent occur during daytime, 49 percent at night.

In the suburbs, burglaries occur as temperatures rise, according to a study by Simon Hakim, Ph.D., professor of economics and director of the Privatization Research Center at Temple University in Philadelphia. Burglaries are highest from May to November, peaking in August and September, when homeowners spend more time outdoors and are away on vacation.

What can you do to deter burglars? Much more than you probably think. Become proactive. Be more cautious. Following are some things you can do that will not only help to keep your belongings intact but will also help you sleep soundly at night. And the cost of protecting your home won't rival the national debt. Which steps to take will depend on several factors: your own anxiety level, the prevalence of crime in your neighborhood, and the value of your possessions, for example.

Use Common Sense

Your first step should be to inspect both the exterior and interior of your house to see how well it is protected from intruders. Play burglar and "case the joint," as they say in crime movies. You want to find weak points, places where a burglar might easily enter, and decide how to better protect those locations. You should give your house a lived-in, protected look that discourages burglars, making them think that entering would not be worth the effort.

When you're away for a long time. If you go away for more than a day, you should take additional steps to protect your home from burglary. When you travel, always have mail and newspaper delivery stopped, or ask a neighbor, friend, or relative to bring them in each day. Also, halt any other regular deliveries and garbage pickup. In fall and winter, arrange for someone to come rake leaves or plow your driveway free of snow and ice, eliminating clues that everyone is away. You might even want to leave a car parked in your driveway or in front of your house to create the impression that someone is at home.

Lights and noise provide good additional deterrents to intruders when you are away. Plan to leave several lights on both inside and outside; you can even put timers on them so they will turn on when it gets dark in the evening. Leave a television or radio on at an audible level. You may also want to turn down the ringer on your telephone so a potential intruder doesn't hear your phone ringing repeatedly when you're supposedly home and taking your calls.

On your answering machine or voice mail, do not leave an outgoing message that you think will be helpful to friends who are wondering where you are. If you say, "Hi! We've gone to visit Bud's parents and we'll be back next Wednesday," you might be giving the go-ahead to a potential burglar who is calling to check whether you are away. Instead, stick to your usual message. If your message system allows you to, you might want to retrieve your messages remotely while you are away. Or you can simply let your callers think you're a bit rude when you don't return their calls immediately. But be aware that multiple beeps on your answering machine might tip off a caller about your absence. Your goal is to keep burglars away by giving the impression that you are home and that your house is safe.

You may want to alert your community's police department about when you will be out of town. If you do, leave the phone number where you can be reached and the phone number of a neighbor who can get in touch with you if something occurs at your home. If you have a home alarm system, make sure to give the police the name and number of a relative or neighbor who has an extra key to your home and who can disarm the alarm if it goes off and the police are contacted.

When you're out for a short time. Whenever you leave your house, even for a short time, be sure you securely close and lock all doors and windows. Lock the door between your attached garage and the house as an extra precaution, and never leave a note outside explaining that you're gone and when you will be back, even if you'll be out for only a few minutes.

If you want to have extra keys to your home in case someone gets locked out, leave them with a relative or neighbor, or hide them in an unusual location. Don't leave them in the garage or under a doormat.

When you go out, it is also smart to leave on some lights and maybe a television, particularly if you'll be out after dark The barking of even a friendly dog can deter some intruders. Alarm company stickers on exterior doors and windows, indicating that your home is protected, also may act as a good deterrent, though a really persistent criminal may not be scared away.

When you're at home. Finally, beware of potential scams. Some thieves will try to work their way into your home by telling you that they are looking for a lost child or dog and asking if they can use your phone. If people want to use your phone, have them wait outside and make the calls for them. Or better yet, if you're in doubt but you sense trouble, discreetly call the police.

You should also never get too friendly with delivery people and repair workers, no matter how nice and helpful they seem. Someone who is hard up for cash or is simply tempted by your possessions could pick up a set of keys that is lying about, have copies made, then enter your home at another time. In fact, you should never put identifying information such as your name, address, or phone number on your key ring, because if you lose it, you will have extended the perfect invitation to a burglar.

If you have young children, be sure they know exactly what to do when someone rings the doorbell. Neither a child nor an adult should ever open a door before knowing who is there, whether it is daytime or evening.

Finally, never leave a front, back, or side door open or any windows ajar even if you are inside the house or in the yard. You may get so busy gardening or doing the wash that you don't hear someone creep in. In a matter of minutes, a professional burglar can make off with some precious valuables.

If somebody does gain entry into your home without your permission, your goal should not be to fight the intruder or to teach him or her a lesson. You should leave the house and get to a phone so you can dial 911. If you can't exit, you should try to lock yourself in a room with a phone and dial 911.

Be sure you convey to any regular visitors to your home the safety precautions you typically follow. Make a list for grand-parents, babysitters, and other people who may stay in your home in your absence. They should know how to lock all your doors and windows when they leave. Run them through a drill to be sure they know how to lock up properly. Leave a neatly compiled list of emergency numbers with them. The list should include the fire and police departments, your heating and air-conditioning company, the electrician, the gas company, the plumber, and at least one neighbor or friend. Also give them all the necessary information about where you're going and how you're getting there.

Tools for Protecting Your Home from Burglary

Landscaping. Plan your landscaping with safety in mind. Trees and shrubs may serve as a hiding place or access point for intruders if they are close to the house or too overgrown, so be diligent about keeping them pruned. It is best to plant a bit away from the house so that, while they add to privacy, your trees and shrubs do not serve as a ladder for entering. Plants with thorns can discourage someone from getting too close and climbing through a window.

Lighting. Providing the right amount of light, both inside and outside, without sending your electric costs soaring requires a tough balancing act, according to Joel Rey-Barreau, consulting director of education for the American Lighting Association in Dallas, Texas, and director of the lighting and design center at the University of Kentucky in Lexington.

When it comes to choosing interior and exterior lighting, your goal is to give your house a lived-in look, but not to make it so bright that it looks like you own stock in the local electric company. Your neighbors won't be pleased with too much wattage glaring through their windows at night.

Start by taking a stroll around the exterior of your house at dusk or at night. You should have sufficient outdoor lighting for all areas so that you can read your watch by that level of light. Then determine whether you and other family members feel comfortable entering the house at night. Specific places to locate lights are along a path to the front door, above the front door, at the sides of the house, at the rear of the house, by any other doors, by the garage whether it's attached or detached, and by any other structures such as a tool shed or playhouse.

There is no "best" type of lighting to choose. The most important consideration may be longevity—how often you have to replace the bulbs. Incandescent lighting is still the standard for easy replacement and low cost, but in the South and West, compact fluorescent lights are popular for the exterior. You can also consider halogen bulbs, which last a very long time and are becoming more reasonably priced. They are more practical, however, for inside rather than outside use.

If you don't want to have to remember to turn lights on and off, you can install photo cells that do the job automatically, according to the amount of natural light that is present. You can buy a photocell for about $10 to $15, but because the lights will stay on all night if you don't turn them off manually, they won't help your electric bill.

Another option is to put some lights on timers, which you can set so they come on randomly rather than every evening at six o'clock. That way burglars will not detect a pattern. The cost of a timer can be as low as $20.

Still another possibility are motion detectors that switch on lights when someone passes through a particular field, such as when a visitor crosses the front yard toward your door. If you're handy with electrical work and understand circuit breakers, you may be able to do the installation yourself. Motion detectors are readily available for as little as $20 to $30 a piece.

New developments in the lighting industry include "smart" bulbs. A Minneapolis company recently patented a bulb that casts a regular, 60-watt light when the switch is flipped once, and becomes a flashing beacon that can be seen from several hundred yards away and in bad weather when the switch is flipped twice. The bulb costs only $20 and lasts up to 2,000 hours.

No matter what type of lights you buy, remember that one very inexpensive way to lower lighting bills is to install dimmers or to turn lights off when you don't need them. You can buy a basic dimmer for under $10 and install it yourself if you're handy. For every 10 percent of incandescent light you dim, you reduce your electrical cost by 10 percent and double the life of your light bulbs.

Finally, when selecting bulbs for either exterior or interior fixtures be sure you get the right ones. Consult labels, and don't hesitate to ask a lighting expert at a lighting or hardware store for help.

You can locate an American Lighting Association retail showroom near your home by calling 800-274-4484.

Locks. Locks for windows and doors can be excellent deterrents, but they must be of a sufficiently high quality to do the trick. Doors should be solid-core wood or steel so they can't be knocked in easily.

Every window should have two pinlocks or clamps to make a potential burglar's task of entering more difficult. You may also want to apply some window film to increase the strength of the glass. It's fairly inexpensive, and you can apply it yourself. Consider installing bars on some windows, like those in the basement or garage, particularly if the windows aren't visible from the street. Make sure the bars have a release mechanism so that you can escape your home quickly if there is a fire.

There are different types of locks you can consider for your doors, depending on your budget and desired level of security.

Key-locking knobs, which cost between $10 and $20, provide minimal protection. Someone who wants to gain entry can succeed by simply giving the knob a good twist.

Standard hardened-steel dead bolts that are one inch in length are also at the low end of the security market price list, selling for between $10 and $20. They are commonly used in tract type housing. These won't be a great deterrent either.

High-security dead bolts, on the other hand, have cylinders that are pick resistant and drill proof, and have keys that only you, the owner, can get from the locksmith who installed the locks. High-security dead bolts are stronger than many other locks and are constructed so that they deter wrenching off the cylinder. And they cannot be drilled through because of the steel rods inside. When properly installed with a high-security strike mounted inside the door jamb, they can also prevent the door from being kicked in. Most high-security dead bolts cost between $125 and $150, but many homeowners and locksmiths consider them a worthwhile investment, according to the Associated Locksmiths of America in Dallas. Ask a friend or a hardware store to recommend a locksmith, or consult your Yellow Pages.

Unless a door has a wide enough pane of glass for you to easily see who's at the door without opening it, consider adding a peephole or a similar type of viewer that enables you to identify visitors.

Doors with large glass present a security risk because the glass can be broken and the door opened. To prevent this, consider replacing regular glass with tempered glass. Be careful to secure sliding glass doors because they are especially vulnerable to break-ins. Insert screws into the upper tracks of the door assemblies to prevent the door, glass, and frame from being raised. You can also install commercially available locks.

If your house is not a brand new one, consider changing the locks. Even though it can be an expensive proposition, it won't be as expensive as it would be to replace your valuables if your house was burglarized. After all, you never know who has had access to the former owner's keys.

It is wise to have just one key for all the doors in your home; this can save you time when you come home late at night and want to enter your house without fumbling with multiple keys. If you lock any doors from the inside, you must keep a copy of the key near each of the doors so you can get out quickly in case of an emergency such as a fire.

Remember that all locks, no matter how secure, are not effective if you don't use them—or if you lose the keys to them. Even if you have a burglar alarm, you should remember to lock your doors. Alarms are designed to let you know when someone has entered the premises, but your initial goal should be to keep uninvited guests out. A good lock should be the first defense, according to the American Locksmith Association.

Security alarm systems. Homes without security systems are more likely to be broken into than homes with them. You might be thinking that an alarm system is too pricey for you. Wrong. It is a myth that such systems are too costly for most homeowners. The average system cost $1,200 in 1998, at least $300 less than the average price at the beginning of the decade, according to the National Burglar and Fire Alarm Association (NBFAA) in Bethesda, Maryland.

Of course, cost will influence your decision about whether to purchase an alarm system and what type to install. You should also take into consideration your real and perceived need for security and the ease of use of particular systems. There's no point in having a system that seems so complicated or is so intimidating that you never turn it on for fear that you may set it off or break it.

You won't need to hire an alarm company to install a lower-end wireless, battery-operated alarm that relies on radio transmitters. You will need to check this type of alarm periodically to make sure it's clean and in working order and that the batteries have sufficient power. These systems are somewhat less reliable than the hardwired systems that most professionals install. Hardwired systems include one or several keypads, window or door contacts, motion detectors, and alarms or sirens, with your specific choices dependent on your pocketbook and the size of your home.

Many of these systems have come down in price because technology is changing and a growing number of companies are installing alarms. In fact, more than 12,000 companies nationwide now sell security systems.

Because of the heightened competition, you may even be lucky enough to pay nothing for installation. The price of an alarm system is often included in the purchase price of a new home, though, of course, the buyer pays for it indirectly. Your homeowners insurance premium might be reduced 2 to 30 percent because you've installed an alarm. You will have to pay a monthly monitoring fee, however. These average $26 per month, or about $310 a year.

If you've decided to install a hardwired system, get at least two or three comparative bids. Reputable companies should belong to an organization such as the NBFAA, indicating that they adhere to high industry standards and are up-to-date on new technology. To accurately compare alarm systems, be sure to ask exactly what the price includes.

When you shop for an alarm system, ask about the types of keypads, the small rectangular boxes that are an integral and critical part of the system. Keypads are typically installed near your main exit doors and also somewhere on an upper story. You punch in your code of numbers on the keypad to "arm" or "disarm" the system, and a flashing red or green light tells you whether the system is on or off. You have a set number of seconds of delay between the time you set or disarm the system and the time you go through the door. Keypads also typically include a "panic" button to hit in case of an emergency.

Your cost of your system will be affected by whether you simply protect windows and doors or whether you add some motion detectors that respond to movement within the house. The downside of motion detectors is that they are easily set off

Key Questions to Ask When Choosing an Alarm System

1. How long has your company been in business? Can you give me some references to call?

2. What is the best type of system for the size and price of my home and our particular family's needs?

3. Will the alarm sound only at my home or also at another location such as the alarm company? (Because of frequent false alarms, few police stations offer this service any more.)

4. Will my phone line go dead when the alarm sounds? If so, should I have backup from radio transmission, a cell phone, or a second phone line?

5. Is there a panic button on the keypad so that I can quickly alert the alarm company if something is awry?

6. How many panic buttons and keypads should I have?

(continued)

Key Questions to Ask When Choosing an Alarm System
(continued)

7. Should the system include smoke, carbon monoxide, and water detectors and how much will these each add to the initial cost and to monthly monitoring fees?

8. What other options exist—glass-break detectors, wired screens, window foil, pressure mats?

9. What is the life expectancy of the system? (In many cases, systems can be expected to last 10 to 15 years.) Is a warranty available?

10. Will I be charged for false alarms from the beginning, or only after a certain number of them have occurred? How high is the false-alarm fee?

11. How easy is it to update the system if I add more windows or doors or decide to take advantage of new technologies?

12. How much security is overkill for a home like ours?

13. Will the company walk family members through the operation of the system so everyone feels comfortable using it?

14. Can additional entry codes be programmed into the system temporarily if workers are coming and going and will need to enter the house when family members are not home? How much does this add to the cost?

15. Should we change the alarm code periodically, and how often?

16. How often do we need to have the company clean and check the system? How much, if anything, does this service cost?

17. Does the alarm system come with a service contract?

18. Is it possible to lease a security system?

when family members or pets move about the house at night. However, they do provide extra security when no one is home.

Whichever system you choose, you need to educate yourself and other family members about all aspects of the system's use. Let the installer walk you through the operation of the system so everyone in the family can be comfortable using it.

Protecting Separate Structures

Any detached unit on your property such as a garage, toolshed, home office, or studio needs the same sort of deterrents as your main structure. Be sure to install locks and an alarm, and use them so that your detached structure won't be vulnerable to theft and won't become a hiding place. Illuminate the separate structure and the path between it and your house. All windows should have tempered glass or laminated plastic glass so they will be difficult to break.

Promoting Neighborhood Safety

Many communities have organized grassroots safety efforts or participate in national programs such as Neighborhood Watch, which brings together neighbors who want to make their communities safe places to live. The effectiveness of Neighborhood Watch has been amply demonstrated. For example, prior to the program's implementation, all but 2 of 15 neighborhoods in Birmingham, Alabama, had experienced burglaries. After the program was in place, 12 of the 15 were burglary free. And Easton, Pennsylvania, saw crime decrease by 29 percent after it started a Neighborhood Watch program. Getting involved in your community's efforts to fight crime will make a difference.

Tracking Inventory

Many local police departments are involved with national and regional identification programs that allow you to borrow an engraving instrument to permanently add an identifying code to valuables like silverware, television sets, and cameras, making it easier for the police department to track and locate items that are stolen.

You may also want to buy a good fire-resistant home safe to store valuables and excess money on your premises. But be aware that it's always safer to put items in a safe-deposit box.

If You Are Burglarized

If you come home to confront a burglar, or if a burglar enters your home while you are there, do your best to avoid him or her. Retreat and quickly call the police. When you return, leave everything as you found it until you figure out just what is missing and the police come and dust for fingerprints. Write down any notes on what happened so you can describe the events to the police officer.

If you return home and find your house has been burglarized, follow the same steps. Call the police. Let them dust for prints. Change all locks and keys, and call your insurance agent to file a claim.

Responding to Natural Disasters

Earthquakes, tornadoes, floods, and hurricanes all require specific safety steps, and it's best to be prepared in advance for the worst of Mother Nature's wrath. You need to get together with your family to decide how you will stay in touch if you are separated by a disaster. The American Red Cross suggests having two meeting places: a location a safe distance from your home in case of fire and a place outside your neighborhood in case you can't return home. You can designate an out-of-state relative or friend as a check-in contact for everyone to call. You should also post all vital emergency telephone numbers by every phone and be sure that every family member who is old enough knows how to shut off water, gas, and electricity at the main switches.

Supplies to Keep on Hand

You should always have certain supplies on hand, particularly if you live in an area prone to natural disasters. The St. Louis Bi-State Chapter of the American Red Cross suggests that emergency supplies of water, food, first aid items, clothing and bedding, and tools be kept in conveniently located and easy-to-carry containers so you can easily access them or take them with you if you are forced to evacuate.

The Red Cross offers the following tips about emergency supplies.

Water. Water should be stored in plastic containers (such as milk jugs) that won't decompose. You should keep at least a three-day supply of water for each member of the family. Each person needs to drink at least two quarts of water a day, and double that amount may be required in a hot environment. Children, nursing mothers, and ill people need even more water. Be sure to change your stored water supply every six months so it stays fresh.

Food. You should store at least three days' worth of nonperishable food that requires no cooking and little or no water for preparation. Foods should also be lightweight in case you need to take them with you. Good items to include are canned meats, fruits, and vegetables; canned juices and soups; staples such as sugar, salt, and pepper; high-energy foods like peanut butter, crackers, and granola bars; vitamins; special foods for infants or elderly people; and comfort foods like cookies, sweetened cereals, and instant coffee and tea bags. Rotate your stored food every six months for freshness.

First-aid supplies. A well-stocked first-aid kit includes sterile adhesive bandages in various sizes; two-inch sterile gauze pads; four-inch sterile gauze pads; hypoallergenic adhesive tape; triangular bandages; two-inch sterile roller bandages; three-inch sterile roller bandages; scissors; tweezers; needles; moistened towelletes; antiseptic ointment; thermometer; tongue depressors; petroleum jelly or another lubricant; safety pins; soap or other cleansing agent; latex gloves; sun screen; nonprescription drugs such as aspirin, anti-diarrhea medicine, and antacid; syrup of Ipecac; laxatives; and activated charcoal, which is recommended by the Poison Control Center to neutralize poisons in the stomach.

Clothing and bedding. In case you cannot return home for one or more nights, have on hand one change of clothing and footwear per person, plus sturdy work boots or other shoes; rain gear; blankets or a sleeping bag for each person; hats and gloves; thermal underwear; sunglasses; bedding such as pillows and sheets; and towels and washcloths.

Tools. Essential tools and supplies to have on hand include a mess kit or two; paper cups and plates and plastic utensils; an emergency-preparedness manual; a battery-operated radio and extra batteries; a flashlight and extra batteries; a miniature TV and batteries; cash or traveler's checks and change; a nonelectric can opener; a utility knife; a fire extinguisher; pliers; tape; a compass; matches stored in a waterproof container; aluminum foil; plastic storage containers; signal flares; paper and pencils; thread and needles of various sizes; a medicine dropper; a shutoff wrench to turn off gas and water; a whistle; plastic sheeting; a map of the area to aid in locating shelters; toilet paper and moist towelletes; hand soap; liquid detergent; feminine supplies; personal hygiene items such as toothbrushes and toothpaste; plastic garbage bags; a plastic bucket with a tight lid to store ice; disinfectant; and household chlorine bleach.

Special items. Depending on your family members' particular needs and interests you may want to include the following: Babies will need diapers, and formula and bottles should be packed even for nursing infants in case they are separated from their mothers. For people who use them, pack prescription medications, extra eyeglasses, and extra contact lenses and solutions.

For all family members have some books, board games, and tapes or CDs.

Your important family documents should be stored together in a waterproof and safe place. These should include your will; insurance policies; contracts; deeds; certificates for stocks and bonds; passports; Social Security cards; immunization records; bank account numbers; credit card account numbers; an inventory of all valuables, including appraisals; and birth, marriage, and death certificates.

Pets supplies. If you have any pets, be sure you stock their supplies, including food, dishes, and toys, as well.

What to Do During the Most Common Disasters

Tornadoes. According to the American Red Cross, tornadoes have been reported in every state. Often there is forewarning that a tornado may occur. The sky grows dark and may turn green, and the National Weather Service may issue a watch or a warning. A "tornado watch" means there is a possibility that a tornado will develop; a "tornado warning" means one has actually been sighted.

If a tornado is approaching, go to the corner of your basement in the direction of the tornado; if you have no basement, take shelter under a piece of heavy furniture in the center of your house. Mobile homes are especially vulnerable to tornadoes, so if you live in one, you should head to a sturdier building whenever tornado weather is brewing.

Hurricanes. Hurricanes bring high winds in excess of 100 miles per hour and cause the worst damage to structures in coastal areas. If you are caught and don't have time to move inland, be sure to board up your windows and protect your doors against the high winds.

Electrical storms. It is wise to protect your home from storm damage. According to the Red Cross, you should consult with a professional about ways to reduce the potential for damage to your roof or garage door. Trim dead or weak limbs from trees to prevent them from falling on your home. Move or secure lawn furniture, outdoor decorations, trash cans, and hanging plants that could be picked up by the wind and become dangerous projectiles.

During an electrical storm you should remain indoors and stay away from windows and doors. You should not use the telephone, and you should turn off electrical appliances.

Floods. You may receive warning about a flood, because they usually take from several hours to several days to develop, according to the Red Cross. Flash floods require faster action because they take only a few hours—or even a few minutes—to develop. A "flood watch" means a flood is possible; a "flood warning" means a flood is occurring and threatens your area.

To get ready, be sure your disaster supplies kit contains all the essentials listed above, especially water, rubber boots, and rubber gloves, and know where you can go if you need to evacuate. Move furniture and valuables to higher floors and fill your car's gas tank to be ready to leave. Listen to the radio or TV, and if you are told to evacuate, do so. If a flash flood warning is given, you must go immediately. Head to higher ground and away from bodies of water. The Red Cross warns that you should not drive around barricades. If your car stalls in rapidly rising waters, abandon it and climb to higher ground.

Earthquakes. Although earthquakes are most frequent in California, other areas of the country are at risk also.

The Red Cross suggests that families in earthquake-prone areas practice for earthquake emergencies at least twice a year by doing "drop, cover, and hold on" drills. Specifically, you should drop under a sturdy desk or table, protect your eyes by pressing your face against your arm, and hold on. If there is no table or desk in the room, sit on the floor against an interior wall away from windows, bookcases, or tall furniture that could fall and injure you.

If an earthquake actually occurs, move only a few steps to a nearby safe place when the shaking begins, then follow the drop, cover, and hold on procedure. Stay indoors until all shaking stops. If you are outdoors, find a clear spot away from buildings, trees, and power lines, and drop to the ground. If you are in a car, slow down, drive to a clear place, and stay in the car until the shaking stops.

Once the shaking has ceased, turn off the gas in your home if you smell it or think it may be leaking. Wait for a professional to turn it back on. Follow instructions on the radio or TV, and be aware that you may experience aftershocks. If you do, follow the same drop, cover, and hold on procedure. The Red Cross suggests using your telephone only to report life-threatening emergencies.

If you live in an earthquake-prone area, you should take care to protect your house and belongings from earthquake damage:

- Install flexible connections on gas and water lines.
- Bolt the frame of your house to the foundation.
- Move all heavy and breakable objects on shelves and bookcases to lower levels.
- Permanently secure light fixtures and ceiling fans to ceiling joists.
- Bolt bookcases, large pictures, china cabinets, and other furniture to wall studs.
- Bolt the hot water heater and gas appliances to floor or wall studs.
- Know the location of all utility shutoffs and how to use them.
- Move chemicals and hazardous objects to low, locked cabinets.
- Secure computers and stereo equipment to desks and shelves using appropriate fastening devices.
- Protect your home from fire. Consult the fire-prevention checklist on pages 47–48.
- Acquire earthquake insurance; most homeowners policies do not provide it.

Fire Safety

According to the National Fire Protection Association (NFPA) in Quincy, Massachusetts, about 80 percent of all U.S. fire deaths occur in homes. In 1997, home fires caused $508,300 in damage every hour. The NFPA attributes the start of most fires to carelessness with products. Many are caused by cigarettes and by children playing with lighters or matches.

To ensure your family's safety, have regular at-home fire drills. The NFPA suggests that you map out an escape plan with specific routes such as a second-story window. If you do choose a second-story window, make sure you have a fire escape ladder positioned underneath. It's important that everyone is able to open all doors and windows. If difficult to do, install relief locks that a child or an elderly person can operate. If someone in your home has a disability, have a contingency plan. Make sure there's a phone in that person's sleeping area or have the person sleep on the first floor. Once you've charted your route, choose a meeting place if, heaven forbid, you ever have to escape. And practice, practice, practice at least twice a year to make sure the exercise becomes automatic. Appoint a family monitor.

If a fire starts, get out of your home fast! Don't turn back for anything. Go to a meeting place and call the fire department. Test doors before opening them. If a door feels hot, use another escape route; if it feels cool, open it carefully. Slam it shut if there is smoke or flames on the other side. To escape from a smoky room, crawl low under the smoke. If you are trapped, use towels to seal cracks around doors to keep out smoke until help arrives. Then go to the window and wave a flashlight to get attention, and if there's a phone in the room, call the fire department and tell them where you are in the house. If your clothes catch fire, stop, drop, and roll to smother the flames.

Is Your Home Well Protected from Fire?

❑ Are your fire alarms fewer than ten years old? Do they work and are they installed on every floor? Are your alarms clean? (Some alarms run on batteries and others on household current. You can install a battery-operated alarm with a drill and screwdriver. Hardwired alarms that plug into you home's electrical system should be installed by an electrician. Many fire departments give out free smoke alarms. Call your local fire department to see if it has such a program.)

❑ Do you have a fire escape plan?

❑ Are there two ways to exit each room in your house?

❑ If you have security bars on windows, do they have quick release devices?

❑ Are flammable liquids stored safely?

❑ Are fuses and circuit breakers the right size?

❑ Are outdoor power supplies safe?

❑ Do you have a working, portable fire extinguisher on a wall in your kitchen? Is it near a door away from your stove, and out of children's reach? Do you check it once a month to see if it works?

❑ Do you stay in the kitchen while food is cooking on the stove?

❑ Is the top of your stove clean and uncluttered?

❑ Are there oven mitts near the stove?

❑ Is a pan lid always within easy reach to squelch a fire?

❑ Are electrical appliances in good condition?

(continued)

Is Your Home Well Protected from Fire?
(continued)

☐ Are electrical loads on outlets properly limited?

☐ If someone smokes, do you have large, deep, nontip ash trays?

☐ Do you have sturdy screens on your fireplaces?

☐ Are space heaters at least three feet from anything that can burn?

☐ Is your chimney clean?

☐ Are matches and lighters out of the sight and reach of children?

☐ Do you avoid running extension cords across doorways or where they can be walked on or pinched by furniture?

☐ Do you know the signs of electrical problems? (Flickering lights, smoke or odd smells, fuses that blow or circuit breakers that are tripped frequently, and frayed or cracked cords are all signs of trouble.)

*Source: Courtesy of the National Fire Prevention Association

Responding to and Preventing Other Emergencies

Other precautions that you can take to make your home safe are to know how to perform cardiopulmonary resuscitation (CPR) and the Heimlich maneuver, which helps choking victims who are still conscious. You should also purchase medicines only in child-resistant packaging and lock up all potential poisons, keeping in mind that many small children are quite clever about getting into even high-up cabinets. Also, always use slip-resistant mats in tubs, ground-fault circuit interrupters to prevent electric shocks, and antiscald faucets at sinks and in showers to protect everybody from excessively hot water.

For more information about unsafe products and practices, contact the Consumer Product Safety Commission in Washington, D.C., by calling 800-638-2772.

Special Considerations for Elderly or Disabled People

It is vital that you know how to care for any senior citizens who spend time in your home on a temporary or long-term basis.

According to John Salmen, author of *The Do-Able Renewable Home,* which is available from the American Association of Retired Persons (AARP), in Washington, D.C., homeowners can use universal design to make their homes accessible to older people and people with disabilities. Universal design involves making accommodations in your home in terms of space and products for people of varying heights and abilities so that your home will be a more comfortable place that they can navigate safely.

To accommodate someone who is in a wheelchair or whose mobility is impaired, you can widen doorways, build ramps, lower cabinets and sinks to waist level, build a shower without doors, install grab bars near the toilet and shower, and move electrical switches lower. If you live in a two-story home, you will need to convert a first-floor room into a bedroom. Any hazardous changes in floor levels that can't be modified should be clearly marked. An outside door can be set with an automatic door opener to make entry easy.

Higher wattage lightbulbs and night-lights will be helpful to people with impaired vision. People with hearing loss will benefit from special electronic devices such as a vibrating alarm clock, amplified television sets and handsets for telephones, and flashing lights that are activated by the doorbell or smoke alarm. People with limited use of their hands require door pulls, locks, and latches that are easier to grasp, turn, and open.

The AARP also offers a booklet entitled *How Well Does Your Home Meet Your Needs?*, which includes a good checklist that will help you learn which areas of your home require improvements.

CHAPTER 3

How to Be a Good Neighbor and Enjoy Your New Surroundings

When you entered the world of homeownership, you undoubtedly discovered that owning your own property is vastly different from renting. Before it was up to the landlord to maintain the property, to keep the building up to snuff by tuckpointing and painting, mowing the grass, and planting and pruning the shrubs and trees.

Now, as a homeowner, you are on your own to maintain the outside of your home, including the lawn, the sidewalks, and the driveway. Now you must become accustomed to following trash and leaf pick-up schedules, removing debris on the street in front of your house, cleaning your windows and gutters, and painting your shutters.

The more you strive to take care of your home, both outside and inside, the more likely your property is to maintain or increase its value. In fact, your property's value may appreciate faster than you thought possible if your neighborhood develops a reputation for being well kept and safe, making it attractive to future homebuyers.

When a New House Becomes Your Home

Regardless of why you moved to your new location or how far you are from your old home, you can expect emotional upheaval. Moving to a new location is a loss. It can take weeks or months—even a year—to complete the grieving process.

Laura L. Herring is a psychologist and relocation expert and is president and CEO of the IMPACT Group, which helps couples and families cope with transition. Herring says that when we make a change such as a move, all of us go through the various stages of grieving described by Elizabeth Kubler-Ross, M.D. Our emotions tend to run the gamut from denial to anger to feelings of guilt and resentment to sadness or even depression. Tears may flow and we may experience emotional burnout. Such feelings can be particularly acute if you moved against your will. You may really miss your old community, your sense of history there, your identity as an active member of the PTA or neighborhood block group. These are all legitimate, normal, and understandable reactions and are part of the grieving and mourning process.

When you move, you have to make conscious changes to reach a new comfort level in your new surroundings. You may have to find a new doctor, hairdresser, dry cleaner, dentist, and veterinarian, and you will need to check out new baby-sitters and schools for your children.

Even under the best circumstances, when your family moves for a good reason, there will always be some confusion and doubt lingering at the back of your mind. You may wonder: Will I be as successful here as I used to be? Will I fit in with the neighbors and the neighborhood? Will I have a best friend again like Suzy next door to the old house? Will I be an insider or will I be treated as an outsider?

You may need time to grieve and to deal with your sense of loss. Herring teaches her clients several ways to cope with these types of emotions.

First, be aware that your emotions are a result of your belief system. If you tell yourself that the experience will be

When a New House Becomes Your Home
(continued)

horrible, it will be. Be aware of why you made the decision to move and hold on to it. Say to yourself, "We made a choice to move to Denver because in the long run it will be best for our family. Sure, there will be change and short-term adjustments. We can choose whether we want to look at them as exciting and wonderful or frustrating and horrible." Accept some truisms. "It *will* be new. I *will* get lost," and manage your expectations by saying, "Of course, I'll get lost, but it will be an adventure."

Second, allow yourself time to mourn. If you get stuck in a negative issue or emotion, give yourself a time limit. Perhaps you're angry because you didn't want to move. You have a right to be angry. But you can choose to stay angry or to be angry for only a limited time—a week, two weeks, perhaps one month. When you've decided how much time you need, tell your loved ones: "You need to know that I'm angry and anxious about this move, and I'm going to be anxious for two weeks. Don't try to change my mind. I have a right to this emotion. Please lay off me for two weeks." If you tell them your plan, the emotion won't seem indefinite to them. Once you have felt your feelings and mourned your loss, you will finally begin to cope more effectively and accept what has happened.

Third, regard the move as an opportunity to reinvent yourself and to focus on your strengths. Make a list of who you are today, what you like about yourself, and what you'd like to change.

Finally, do something symbolic to remember your old neighborhood if it makes you feel better. Plant a tree or make a contribution to a worthy cause, or compile a scrapbook.

Remember that other family members are grieving as well. Talk with them and tell them that moving is a natural part of life as is any loss or change. Don't forget that you are a role model for your children, and what they learn will influence how they will cope with other losses in the future.

Neighbors Make the Neighborhood

Neighborhoods and neighbors are very important in the human psyche. Whether you live in a tiny bungalow in a crowded city like Los Angeles, in a quaint cottage amid birch and dogwood trees acres from your nearest neighbor, or in a condominium where dozens of other units are in the same building, you probably yearn for a sense of community. Even when neighbors are separated physically by walls and grass and driveways, there is no reason for a psychological chasm between them. Healthy exchanges with your neighbors can give you a sense of place in your new home.

Some planned communities promote neighborhood camaraderie by providing a "common house," a place where neighbors share a variety of facilities such as a kitchen, meeting hall, game room, and courtyard. Neighborliness gives streets that human touch. Taking a cake or pie to someone's door is a simple gesture of goodwill that says, "I'm glad to be here and to live next to you. I'm here if you need me." This type of camaraderie makes neighborhoods stronger and better. The motto of the Neighborhood Stabilization Team of St. Louis sums it up best: "You don't have to move to live in a better neighborhood." In other words, a neighborhood is as good as its neighbors.

You can't pick your neighbors, but you can do everything you can to get along with them. Common courtesies among neighbors strengthen bonds in any community.

For example, don't let your dog go on your neighbors' lawns, and when you take him for a walk, clean up after him. Compliment a neighbor on her pretty yard or the nice-color paint on her shutters. Ask a neighbor's advice: What type of flowers do you think would look best along this path? Who are the good babysitters in the neighborhood? Do you know a good plumber? Offer to take in a neighbor's newspapers and mail when he's on vacation and accept his offer to do the same for you. Give him your phone number for use in case of emergency.

Be available to help. Tell your neighbor, "Yes, you may give my number to the alarm company so I can respond if your alarm goes off while you're not home." Offer to help your neighbor to carry something heavy into her garage or to load a broken lawn mower into the back of her truck. If a petition needs to be signed concerning street lighting, offer to help circulate the petition.

Talk about forming a babysitting co-op. If certain trees divide your property from your neighbor's, offer to split the cost of pruning, fertilizing, or replacing them. If you're having a party, alert the police to post No Parking signs across the street from your home so your guests don't block both sides of the street with their cars.

Be friendly. Wave to people who walk past your house or see you on the street. If you're the outgoing type, talk to your neighbors, asking questions about what they do, whether they have children or pets, what the schools are like, and who the better teachers and principals are. Learn about play facilities, after-school sports activities, churches, preschools, and after-school care programs.

Don't store materials of any type in your yard—this can make it look unkempt. Don't have an excessive number of pets. Invite a few nearby neighbors to your house for coffee or a barbecue, and during their visit, ask them questions about themselves and their children. They may return the invitation.

Find out about the idiosyncrasies of your neighborhood. There are always good stories to share because people love to gossip, but take what you may hear about certain neighbors with a grain of salt. Form your own opinions about everyone without being too judgmental. You don't know what others may be saying about you someday.

There is a push toward a new neighborliness in many areas. Consider one man's story. One morning, he accidentally left his brand-new briefcase at the bus stop in his neighborhood. It contained all his important papers. He thought he would never see it again, even though his name was written on an address book inside. On a prayer and a hunch, he went back to the bus stop to see if it had been returned, and he even called the public bus company. No luck. The next day, a man who lived at the end of his block dropped off the briefcase at his front door. He had met the man at a neighborhood watch meeting.

Neighborhood Groups

There are other practical reasons to know your neighbors. For example, neighborhood security can be improved through neighborhood watch groups, block parties, and trustees meetings.

A community that bands together and forms a Neighborhood Watch helps reduce the risk of crime, prepares residents to respond to suspicious activity, provides a conduit for information about the community, enables neighbors to get to know one another, and makes the neighborhood more livable and desirable. It is not necessary to turn inward to protect yourself in a home set up like a fortress because these groups allow you to turn outward to the community to join with others to ward off crime.

Whether or not you live in a high crime area, neighborhood groups help instill a greater sense of community by putting the neighbor back into the neighborhood. Neighborhood groups bring people together for a common cause and pump new life into communities.

Neighborhood Watch groups or block clubs are membership organizations that appoint a captain to serve as liaison between residents and police. The captain schedules activities; supplies a core group of coordinators with information and lists of members; distributes maps of the area and a neighborhood buzz book with names, addresses, and telephone numbers; sets up a telephone chain; distributes information; and greets new neighbors and encourages them to join the neighborhood association. In many areas where immigrants might be moving, printed materials may be translated into Polish, Spanish, Vietnamese, or other languages.

When a block group is the nucleus of a neighborhood, everyone plays a part in safety. You learn your neighbors' names

Safety Reminders from Your Block Captain

- Make sure your home is secure. You know the weak areas, so tighten them up now.

- Know your neighbors. Go meet the people who live behind and next door to you. Exchange names and telephone numbers. Encourage your neighbors to call 911 if they see anyone or anything on your property that "just doesn't look right." Let them know you will do the same for them—and do it.

- Add exterior lighting. Increasing lighting on and around buildings not only makes the neighborhood more pleasant and safe, but it also might help someone to observe and to be able to accurately describe a suspicious person to the police.

- Pay attention to noises. A loud thumping sound could be your neighbor's door being kicked in. Barking dogs are an alert that something is happening. Check it out. If in doubt, call 911. Many people in the neighborhood may have burglar alarms. If you hear one sounding, call 911 and then watch so you can observe anything unusual.

- Give police officers the information they need. You can tell the dispatcher you do not want the officers to come to your home. If the patrol car has a phone, you may be able to tell them where a weapon or drugs were quickly hidden or which direction the perpetrators ran. You can even give them a description without having a face-to-face conversation.

- Be sure your address is clearly visible at both the front and rear of your home.

- Remember that you are not alone. Together neighbors can make a dramatic difference in community safety.

Published by the Mayor's Neighborhood Stabilization Team, City of St. Louis.

and the cars they drive. If you spot suspicious activity, you know to call the police or the appropriate person or agency. Some groups have a neighborhood safety signal such as raising and lowering a flag or turning off and on a certain light. Other clubs start a phone chain for reporting emergency information and for calling certain people daily to check on them. Also, some neighborhood organizations do a residential security survey to make sure all homes are safe and crime resistant. They check to see that there are proper locks on all windows and doors and that smoke and burglar alarm systems are in working order.

Typically, neighborhood groups work with the police, elected officials, government agencies, social service organizations, community groups, and individuals. This is all about teamwork.

Some neighborhood groups feature monthly talks on personal safety and defense, child abuse, child safety, cons and fraud, latch-key kids, abuse of the elderly, home security, and burglary prevention.

Neighborhood Stabilization's "Team Sweep" project in St. Louis encourages teams of young people ages 9 to 17 and their adult supervisors to maintain blocks and alleys and keep them clean year-round. The project not only keeps the area looking shipshape, but it also helps instill a feeling of pride in those kids responsible for the work.

Success stories of neighborhood groups proliferate. The city of St. Louis cites one block that experienced burglaries, break-ins, suspected drug use, and nuisance crimes including public drinking and the playing of loud car stereos. A group of residents was determined to do something about it. They got information from the Neighborhood Stabilization Team, chose a meeting date, and made up a flyer and distributed it to everyone's door. The residents who attended the meeting gave their input, and a plan of action was drafted. Police began to make arrests and deal with nuisance crimes. The city improved property conditions by starting periodic health and building inspections and towing derelict cars.

Two years after the first meeting, calls for the police have decreased. The block unit is going strong and is still working to maintain safety. Now that the area is safer, the block unit has shifted its concern to other issues and has begun to sponsor alley cleanups and youth activities. The area's reputation has improved, and the neighborhood has become a desirable place to live.

Organizing a Neighborhood Gathering

When you move in, some of your more hospitable, gracious neighbors may spot the moving truck in front of your new home and bring over a jar of homemade jam, a plate of brownies, or an invitation to your entire family for dinner or lunch. Such niceties will be long remembered. But unless you have young children who play outdoors, getting to know your more reticent neighbors will be much more difficult because many families have such busy—even chaotic—lives.

Some neighborhoods organize block parties for just this reason—families should get to know each other. If your neighborhood does not already have a tradition of bringing everyone together once or twice a year, perhaps you can start one.

First, make a list of everyone who lives on the block or in the immediate vicinity. You can define the boundaries in any way you please. Once you have your neighbors' names, addresses, and phone numbers, write a letter explaining your idea. State that you want to have a block gathering on a certain date—possibly on a holiday like the Fourth of July or Labor Day when many people are home. Ask everyone to consider participating in a planning meeting at your home or in a public spot such as a coffee bar or library. If you get little or no response, take the initiative and call people, asking them if they would like to help organize the gathering.

Residents of one neighborhood that had stopped having its annual fete years before decided that a Sunday evening barbecue in early September, when people would be back from vacation, would be appealing. The party organizer asked each family to contribute $5 to $10 per family and to bring hors d'oeuvres or a dessert and a six-pack of soda or beer or a pitcher of lemonade. The money went toward hot dogs and hamburgers, condiments, buns, paper plates and cups, plastic cutlery, and charcoal for grilling. A central location was chosen for the party, and a rain date was also set. The party ended up being a huge success. Many families found that they had a lot in common with their neighbors and newfound friends.

Perhaps you will want to plan another event just for children. Or maybe one family with a large yard will decide to host the next event, hoping that the ball will be picked up by other families in subsequent years. Whatever the theme, menu, and location, the bottom-line purpose should remain the same. A neighborhood gathering is an event that fosters camaraderie and encourages an enhanced measure of togetherness, caring, and safety.

A Quiz for Conscientious Neighbors

Neighborliness involves more than just being friendly and helpful. It also involves following a prescribed set of rules on safety inspections, yard-waste disposal and trash pick up, parking cars and commercial vehicles, noises and disturbances, and building permits. Most areas publish a list of services that is disseminated to new residents. In addition, some cities publish a question-and-answer guide with names, agencies, and phone numbers of the proper contacts to turn to if a problem persists and needs correcting. Perhaps your neighborhood group can distribute a list with questions like the following.

1. My neighbors are putting their trash in the yard-waste-only dumpster. To whom should I report them?

2. Someone was evicted and the trash is still on the street. Who is responsible for picking it up?

A Quiz for Conscientious Neighbors
(continued)

3. The house next to mine is in disrepair. Is the owner required to fix it up?

4. My neighbor's backyard is full of trash. Is this illegal?

5. My neighbor's grass is three feet high. Doesn't he have to mow it?

6. I've got problems with the renters living next to me. Who can I call to find out who owns the property?

7. I have a horn-honking problem on my block. Should I call the police when the horns get started?

8. My neighbors are washing their car on the street and playing loud music. How do I get them to stop?

9. My neighbors are constantly working on their cars, and they leave trash, oil, and other stuff laying about. It's gross. Are they allowed to do this?

10. I think my neighbors may be selling drugs. Who do I call to get it stopped?

11. It's past 10 PM, and kids are playing in the street. What can I do?

12. There's a party going on down the street and I can hear the noise loudly in my house. Is it the job of the police to tell them to quiet down?

13. There's a gang of kids hanging out on my block. What can I do without getting into trouble with them?

14. I've seen someone who doesn't live in the neighborhood dumping trash in my dumpster. What can I do?

15. I'm going away on vacation. Can I have the police watch my house?

16. Does the city engrave valuables?

(continued)

A Quiz for Conscientious Neighbors
(continued)

17. Does the city provide free crime-prevention appraisals?

18. What is the curfew for children?

19. Kids on my block who should be in school are playing outside instead. What should I do?

20. There is graffiti on some buildings. Who is supposed to remove it?

21. My dumpster is full and the sanitation workers won't empty it. Who should I call?

22. There is a pothole on my street that could stop a tank. How do I get it fixed?

23. We're having sewer problems in our alley? Who do we call?

24. A street light is out in front of my house. Which city department is responsible for fixing it?

25. A huge tree branch has fallen in front of my house. Am I responsible for having it removed? If not, who is?

26. How do I contact my alderman or city council member?

27. I've heard there are free trees and flowers available from the city. How do I get some?

28. Where can I get a free smoke alarm?

29. I've heard that the city will replace the sidewalk in front of my house and split the cost with me. Who do I call?

30. I've heard the city is giving away houses for a dollar. How do I find out more?

31. How can I buy abandoned property?

Published by the Mayor's Neighborhood Stabilization Team, City of St. Louis.

Budgeting and Financial Planning

A Balancing Act

Here's a pop quiz: What's the most cost-effective way to care for your home and meet other expenses? If you're not sure, you have lots of company. Most new homeowners substantially underestimate the costs of owning.

Take time out for a reality check. Don't think for a minute that paying for your home once you're in it will be like a lazy float down a quiet river. Sure, you were able to get a mortgage and to buy your own house. And you couldn't be happier. You like your new neighborhood. You have a short commute. Your children are in decent schools and friends are nearby. Your house would be easy to afford if nothing changed, if insurance prices and property taxes stayed the same, if there was no such thing as inflation, and you didn't have to sink another dime into decorating your home. But in the real world, it's another story.

And if you have the fantasy that a long-lost relative will leave you a million dollars, that a tidal wave of coins will pour from a slot machine at some fancy new Las Vegas casino, or that Ed McMahon will knock on the door with a check from Publishers Clearing House, keep dreaming.

Owning a home usually is more economical than renting. Although a home is likely to be the biggest purchase of your life, it's historically been a good investment, and the tax benefits are a boon. So pat yourself on the back for being so smart and savvy. But don't get cocky.

Rethinking Your Finances as a Homeowner

Owning a home can be a dream come true, but experts warn that you should be careful not to let it turn into a financial nightmare by spending money too freely and winding up deeper in debt. Human nature is such that we love to buy new things—furniture, electronics, fast and expensive cars. But now that you're a homeowner, you should be conservative with purchases. Pay off outstanding debts and continue to invest some money for your children's college education and your own retirement. That way your money can grow. Build up an emergencies fund that you can tap into if you have to replace your heating or if your roof leaks. A savings safety cushion equal to three to six months of income is good to have. It makes sense to save 1 to 3 percent of the purchase price of your home on an annual basis. For a $150,000 home, that would mean adding $1,500 to $4,500 to your nest egg each year.

When deciding how you'll juggle your finances as a homeowner, you can never ask too many questions. Do you think you've accounted for all your expenses? There are ongoing costs above and beyond the monthly mortgage payment: There are repairs, never-ending taxes, insurance, and property maintenance. There are utilities such as telephone, cable, gas, water, and electricity. And don't forget costs like garbage collection, furniture, decorating, and emergencies such as illness or the loss of a job.

Have you decided whether you can live without living room furniture or other amenities for a while? Keep in mind that you may have to ratchet down your lifestyle in order to afford your new home. You may have to forgo that weekend fishing trip, your health club membership, those delicious steak dinners, or your weekly date at the movies.

Budgeting

In order to afford your home, you must keep your current debt low. You must continue to pay credit card balances, student loans, and car installments along with your new monthly mortgage payment. And money will continue to flow out via debit cards, credit cards, preauthorized withdrawals, and cash and check purchases. If you go through your money like someone with a cold goes through tissues, you may need more careful planning to handle all the new and potentially steep expenses bombarding you at once.

This means creating a budget, something that has become a dying art. Preparing one is as important as planning your wedding or figuring out how to get a mortgage.

What a Budget Can Do for You

Budgeting is a way to learn more about how to save and how to make your money grow for you, how to invest for the future, how to sock away dollars for retirement, how to finance your or your children's education, and how to be ready to replace or repair your air-conditioning, heating, roof, or siding.

Budgeting is also about learning how to tailor your savings to your spending needs and how to take into account your risk tolerance. It's important to see how sensitive your pocketbook may be to increases in property taxes or insurance. A budget serves this purpose because you can make calculations based on your current rates and on what you could expect to pay if rates were to climb. Finally, a detailed budget helps you see how you can reallocate funds if an emergency occurs.

An emergency forced Joe and Mary Newhart (not their real names) to budget. Mary and Joe, both of whom held good jobs, were down on their luck. When Joe got in a serious car accident and was out of work for a time, their precarious financial position became worse, and they had no emergency funds squirreled away. So Mary learned how to budget what limited income the couple did have.

First, Mary turned to a credit counselor with a nonprofit agency, who helped her to set goals and priorities, prepare a monthly budget, then track expenses and save money. When Mary took control of her daily finances, she was able to balance income and outgo. Within a year, she had paid off her credit cards and had accumulated four months' worth of money in the bank to pay bills. She was also maxing out her employer-sponsored retirement plan, a 401(k). The employer matches her 401(k) contribution, and earnings on her investment are tax deferred until she pulls the money out for retirement.

A budget tells you in black and white where your money comes from, when it comes in, and how it's being spent. It highlights both *fixed expenses*—your mortgage, insurance, car, and tuition payments and other expenditures that remain the same each month—and *variable expenses*, which include utilities, food, and clothing. You can create a weekly, monthly, or annual budget—whatever time frame makes it easiest to adhere to your plan.

It doesn't matter whether you do your budget on graph paper, on a sheet of typing paper, on a fancy spreadsheet on your computer, or on one of the worksheets at the back of this chapter. The bottom line is the same: It's important to keep good records. If you have access to a computer, you can acquire a program that will help you plan your budget and track income and expenses. Quicken and Microsoft Money are two of the better and more user-friendly budgeting programs.

How to Get Started on a Budget

Budgeting is really all about planning. You plan what you're going to wear to work each day, you plan meals, you plan your weekend. A budget is a money plan that will enable you to carry out your other plans. It helps organize your financial life in a rather uncomplicated way.

Some Quick Budgeting Tips at a Glance

1. Keep a file of household bills and choose a date, time, and place each month to pay them and balance your checkbook. It's best to pay the ones with the highest interest rates first, or at least pare them as much as possible. Of course, certain bills must be paid in full and on time each month, such as your house payment and utilities. Simultaneously, maintain a schedule of when certain bills need to be paid that don't come on a regular basis, such as property taxes and insurance premiums.

2. Avoid sales at the mall. Such purchases may only lead to more debt and will completely destroy your budgeting, unless it's a holiday and you've saved a specific amount of money for gifts. If that's the case, still try to stay within your budget.

3. If you get a pay increase, take money out of your paycheck before you spend it. You are not taxed on money from your paycheck that you put into a 401(k). One of the best ways to save is to put money into your 401(k) because most companies will match the entire amount or give you a percentage of your contribution. It's free money, so take advantage of it. Then, if you have any money left, try to pay off as many pressing bills as possible. If you've kept good records, it should be easy to determine what bills need to be paid as soon as possible.

Before you begin crunching numbers, first draft a mission statement. Define your goals in 25 words or less, thinking about your lifestyle, what possibilities may derail your goals, and what you may have to change about your lifestyle to meet your goals. Consider what you want to accomplish with your budget, what you can afford, and what your priorities are. Set both short-term goals, like paying monthly bills on time, and long-term goals, such as buying a second car.

Next, attach a money amount to each goal. For example, if you want to buy an inexpensive used car for your teenage son so he can get to and from his after-school job, you might need to set aside $2,400. This may mean socking away $200 a month for an entire year. If you put this money into a savings account, you can pay cash for the car, and you won't have to throw money away on interest.

Now list and add up all sources of income, such as dividends, salary, tips, and gifts. Then, write down and add up all fixed and variable daily, monthly, and yearly expenses. To ensure that you cover all your bases, consult the chart at the end of this chapter and let your budgeted savings reflect the goals you have just developed. Make sure that you budget for adequate property, medical, disability, and life insurance. Remember that fixed expenses can change at some point, but you do have to pay a fairly consistent amount on these items each month. And incidentally, while property taxes are usually part of your mortgage, some mortgage providers will allow you to put the property tax money in an escrow account to pay it once a year. This may be best if you receive a lump sum of money such as a sales bonus once a year.

Next, subtract expenses from income. If your expenses exceed your income, think about where to cut. The best place to start is with your variable expenses. You may also need to modify the goals you developed at the beginning of the budgeting process.

If you overuse credit, pay bills late, pay only the minimum on credit cards, use savings to pay bills, are on the top of each collection agency's list, or avoid buying medication you need because it's too expensive, your budget will help you put a stop to these risky and expensive practices. Budgeting will enable you to shore up your bottom line and pay back your debt.

Borrowing and Using Credit Wisely

Ironically, debt can help you achieve a modicum of financial security. Your mortgage is a prime example. You acquire a good credit rating by paying interest and by paying it consistently and on time each month. It is this good credit that may help you get a loan for something else in the future.

You build credit also by paying bills on time. If you need to repair bad credit or clean up your record, start now. It takes seven years for unfavorable credit information to be dropped from your credit report. Bankruptcy remains on your credit report for ten years.

The time may come when you want or need to borrow money. You might have to pay for an emergency hospitalization. Perhaps you want to add on another bathroom, or maybe your basement floods and you need to waterproof it.

Deciding Whether to Borrow

Before you run to the nearest lender, sort out your reasons for seeking the loan, and look at your budget. Ask yourself some pertinent questions to determine whether you really need the loan: Can you pay for the expenses out of savings? Is the project worth the additional expense of interest? What if your financial situation changes during the course of the loan? What impact will borrowing more money have on your budget and on the rest of your family?

Let's assume you want to redo your kitchen floor and buy new appliances. Can you afford to assume more debt? You think you can, but you'll have to have your project financed. There are ways to figure out whether you and the bank think that you can afford to pay for your remodeling on a monthly basis. There's a simple Debt-to-Income (DTI) ratio that lenders use. Here's how it works:

Enter your total monthly expenses	$_____
Add the estimated monthly payment for the remodeling project	+$_____
Total	=$_____
Divide total by your gross monthly income (Divide) $_____	
DTI	%=_____

Each lender has it's own acceptable DTI percentage. If you find 50 percent is acceptable and your DTI is 40, you are in good standing and your loan should be okayed. If you find that your DTI is 65 percent and your lender accepts a 50 percent maximum, you'll need to find another financing option or delay the project until you save more funds.

Or, you can cut back on your project and do only what you can currently afford. You think you can afford to redo the floor and buy a new refrigerator, but the rest of the appliances will have to wait. To figure out the maximum monthly payment you can afford for the remodeling, multiply your monthly gross income amount by the lender's maximum DTI allowance. Then, subtract your current total monthly expenses, excluding your remodeling project payment:

Gross monthly income	$ _____
Lender's DTI ratio	× _____
Subtotal	=$ _____
Total monthly expenses	− _____
Maximum affordable payment	=$ _____

If the last line is in the negative category, forget borrowing from that lender.

If your percentages aren't up to snuff, you may want to consider a debt consolidation loan, a loan that incorporates all your current debts, plus the cost of the new project, into one loan. All your debt is rolled into one lump sum, and you need to make only one payment, resulting in less paperwork for you. The interest rate on a consolidation loan is often lower than the interest rates you may be currently paying for each separate debt. By consolidating, you may save money each month.

Procuring a Loan

Procuring a loan can be every bit as difficult as getting a home mortgage. The financing process can be intimidating, but good preparation can eliminate some worry. Here's what to have with you:

Personal information. Bring your Social Security number and driver's license, home addresses for the past two years, and, if applicable, divorce decree or separation agreement.

Income. You will need your most recent pay stubs; documentation of supplemental income; names, addresses, and phone numbers of all employers for the past two years; W-2 forms from the past two years; if you are self-employed or are a commissioned salesperson, copies of the past two years' tax returns with all schedules and a year-to-date profit and loss statement that has been signed by an accountant.

Records of real estate you own. Bring the names, addresses, and phone numbers of all mortgage lending institutions you have borrowed from in the past seven years. If you own rental property, bring copies of leases, the past two years' tax returns, and market value estimates, if possible.

A list of liquid assets. Have all names, addresses, phone numbers, and account numbers relating to your bank accounts. Bring copies of any notes receivable, and know the value of other assets such as cars and household goods, the cash value of life insurance policies, and the amount of vested interest in retirement funds.

A list of liabilities. You will need the names and account numbers relating to all installment loans and credit cards, and the balance and current monthly payment amount for each. Bring records of your alimony or child-support payment amounts, if applicable.

Types of Loans

Retirement loans. In a pinch, you can borrow from your 401(k), but if you do, there are several strings attached. First of all, when you remove money from your account, it's no longer compounding and growing. If the economy is strong, you might miss a few years of high returns. Worse, if you resign from your company or get fired, you have to repay the loan in full according to the plan's rules, and usually within 60 days. If you default, you risk being taxed on the loan and owing a penalty for withdrawing the funds before you are 59½ years old. Finally, there is no tax deduction on the interest you pay on this type of loan. If you do access your 401(k) as a source of money for a new home or to pay down debt, pay it back as soon as possible.

Home equity loans. Once you've paid a substantial amount of money on your mortgage, a home equity loan can help you to build up your consumer credit if it's shaky. Home equity loans can be used for home improvements or for debt consolidation, and interest on them is tax deductible up to a certain point. Be careful, however, if you default on a home equity loan, you can literally lose the roof over your head.

There are two types of home equity loans: line of credit and lump sum. Interest rates on these do vary, so shop around for the best rate.

You may want to set up a home equity line of credit to draw from in case you lose your job or have emergency expenses. Or perhaps you plan to paint the inside and outside of your home, fix a major plumbing problem, or remodel your basement. You are allowed to draw funds from this loan as needed; it's much like using a checking account. You have to repay the money you withdraw plus interest. The upside of a line of credit is that you borrow only the amount you need. The downside is that these loans are often pegged to the prime rate, which may move up and down, making budgeting difficult.

Home equity financing that gives you funds in a lump sum also allows you to borrow on the equity you have built up in your home. (Equity is the value of your home minus the outstanding balance on any mortgages.) The interest rate on a lump-sum loan is usually fixed, so it will remain the same each month.

Don't go overboard on your home equity debt. It may seem like an ideal way to finance a home renovation or to pay for college tuition, but if home prices fall, you may have to dip into savings to repay the loan when you sell your home someday. Also, most financial advisors advise that you steer clear of the 125 percent loans, which allow you to borrow up to 125 percent of the market value of your home. You may risk losing your home if its market value drops. Limit your home equity borrowings so that a price decline won't wipe out your equity. After all, you'll want to walk away with some extra cash in your pocket when you finally sell the old homestead.

Second mortgages. A second mortgage is a collateral mortgage that usually has a higher interest rate than the initial loan. The interest you pay on it is tax deductible, which pares down the cost of borrowing. Generally, a second mortgage has a higher interest rate than a home equity loan. To compare the two loan options, you must look not only at interest rates, but also at financing fees, including application fees; points; loan origination fees; and service fees for title search, survey appraisal, credit check, and legal work.

No-equity loans. Even if you don't have equity built up in your home, you may be able to procure a no-equity debt consolidation loan to lower overall debt. The interest on these loans is tax deductible. The Federal Housing Administration (FHA) offers no-equity loans that can be used to finance property improvements, but the paperwork on these can be terribly slow.

Margin loans. If you own stocks and other securities, you may be able to procure a margin loan. Some lenders allow you to borrow up to 50 percent of the value of your stocks or up to 90 percent of the value of Treasury securities, and the interest rates are typically low. The interest you pay on margin debt is tax deductible. However, there is one major downside. If the value of your stocks plummets, you might need to come up with cash to make up the difference or be forced to sell your holdings when the market is low.

Personal loans. There are many types of personal loans. Examples of these include debt consolidation loans or unsecured lines of credit based on earning capacity or net worth. Interest rates depend on your credit history and, in the case of a secured loan, on the value of the collateral to which it is tied. If you do secure a loan with savings, remember that you cannot spend what's in your account.

Credit card loans. Using credit cards is the worst way to borrow money because typically interest rates are sky-high. And it's too easy to get credit cards. The credit card determines the amount you can borrow. If you turn to this type of loan for a quick fix, try to pay it back immediately before the interest (which is not deductible) wipes you out.

Exercising Mortgage Repayment Options

You can pay down your mortgage more quickly in order to build up the equity in your home. One way to reduce your loan is to make a 13th payment each year. This will reduce the time it takes to pay off your home and can save you thousands of dollars. But first make sure there is no prepayment penalty. You can also increase your regular payment by as much as 15 percent. Before you decide to increase the size or number of your payments, remember to take into account the fact that mortgage interest is tax deductible.

If you want to have more spending money, you can refinance your mortgage. What you do in essence is take on a new mortgage to pay off your existing mortgage. Excess funds will be available to you as a result.

If you can get a new mortgage with interest that is a percentage point or two less than that of the original mortgage, it makes sense to refinance. For example, if you have a five-year-old, $100,000 mortgage at a 30-year fixed rate of 8 percent, your payments are about $734. If you refinance at 7 percent for another 30 years, your payments drop to $633. As if you were on a quick diet, you have shed $100 of expenses each month. You can invest this money so it will grow or will be available in case of an emergency.

Mortgage providers send out a flood of direct mailings to entice consumers to refinance. Many push deals that require minimal fees and no points. That makes refinancing attractive for consumers who are saddled with high-rate mortgages, who want to consolidate other debts under the lower interest rate and tax deductibility of a mortgage, or who want to take advantage of low rates to borrow for their children's college tuition or to fund major home improvements. But don't be too anxious to jump on the refinancing bandwagon. Before you refinance, be certain that

Ten Ways to Avoid a Money Mishap

1. Know your financial worth.

2. Have a gauge of your expenses.

3. Pay off high-interest debt first.

4. Have an emergency fund equal to three to six months' income.

5. Know your financial goals. Type them up and post them on your refrigerator door or on a bulletin board.

6. Have enough life, medical, disability, and homeowners insurance.

7. Have an up-do-date will.

8. Keep careful financial records.

9. Plan for retirement as soon as you start earning money full-time.

10. Understand the tax benefits that are available to you.

you'll stay in your house long enough to recoup the loan's closing costs by making the new, lower monthly payments.

How to Get Back into Financial Shape If You Slip

You're up to your eyeballs in loans that you can barely repay, and you have tapped out your home equity. What do you do? First, you should pare down your debts by paying off those with the highest interest rates. This will have the biggest and fastest impact on reducing your debt. Experts recommend paying off consumer loans first, starting with credit card balances, which have an average interest rate of 18 percent. Then put the money you save into an IRA, a college fund, your 401(k), or stocks.

If you're still burdened by the weight of your debts, don't hesitate to contact your creditors to find out if you can arrange to pay late or in smaller increments. Most creditors will work with you as long as you agree to pay off the debt at some point.

If you cannot control your spending, get professional financial planning help. There are clinics and nonprofit groups that charge little or nothing to people in crisis. Look in the phone book or ask your lender for a recommendation. When you do find a financial advisor or counselor, ask for his qualifications. Are you okay discussing finances with him? Does he explain things to you and answer your questions? Does he understand your goals and needs?

You and the credit counselor will draft a strict debt-management regimen and make sure you stick to it. Sometimes the discipline of having someone looking over your shoulder is all that you need. The credit counselor may also be able to negotiate some breathing room or better terms for you to pay back your debts.

Credit card debt can be the most debilitating financial web to be caught in, and it is also the most common. So avoid credit

For budget or credit counseling contact:

Fannie Mae
800-732-6643

House America Counseling Center
800-577-3732

National Foundation for Consumer Credit (which can refer you to a Consumer Credit Counseling Service office near you)
301-589-5600

card debt at all costs. Cut up your credit cards, and when you recover from your financial ills, only use one. Keep it simple. Do you really need multiple charge cards and interest rates? When you do apply for a credit card, shop for the lowest rate. And avoid paying even the lower rate; don't charge more than you can pay off completely at the end of the month.

Remember that if you weren't able to afford your home, the lender would not have given you a loan in the first place. Still, if you think you cannot pay your mortgage, contact your lender and work out a solution.

Whatever tactics you use to curb your spending, monitor yourself every month or find a buddy whom you trust and monitor one another. It's scary when you consider that personal bankruptcies are piling up faster than credit card offers. Don't run away from problems. Face them head on and you can avoid bankruptcy and foreclosure.

Credit. Before issuing a loan, a lender will run a credit check on you to verify your credit worthiness. According to the Fair Credit Reporting Act, you are entitled to a summary of your own credit report. You may want to check your credit file if you aren't sure of your rating, if you are refused credit, or if you plan to apply for a large loan such as a second mortgage.

You may obtain a copy of your credit report for a nominal fee by contacting one of the national bureaus. In your request letter, include your full name, birthdate, Social Security number, current address, former addresses for the past two to five years, the name of your current employer, a photocopy of your driver's license or a phone bill showing your current address, and a photocopy of your Social Security card.

Some areas have a local credit bureaus affiliated with one of the big national firms that will sell you the same credit report over the counter, in person. Check your local yellow pages under Credit Reports. You can even order a merged, three-bureau report online at <www.creditreport.com>.

If you see incorrect information in the report, you have the right to challenge it, and you should do so in writing immediately, listing the most serious discrepancies first. Try to deal with each questionable item individually. The Fair Credit Reporting Act requires credit reporting agencies to remove all inaccuracies.

 National Credit Bureaus

Equifax
P.O. Box 105873
Atlanta, GA 30348
800-685-1111

Experian
P.O. Box 2104
Allen, TX 75013-2104
888-397-3742

Trans Union Corporation
P.O. Box 390
Springfield, PA 19064-0390
800-888-4213

For additional information on credit report rights, contact the Federal Trade Commission office.

To improve your credit rating, close inactive credit card accounts, and don't apply for too many loans simultaneously—it sends up a red flag. Take advantage of automated payment options—companies will withdraw payments from your checking or savings account automatically. It you tend to pay late, this is a good way to keep your bill paying current. Try to avoid late fees because all of them show up on your credit report. If you incur a late fee because you were out of town or you didn't receive the bill on time, report it to the company so it doesn't go on your credit report. And check your credit report from time to time so you can correct mistakes.

Saving and Investing

Surprise! You've budgeted, paid down your debts, and curbed your spending, and lo and behold, there's money left over. Your first inclination may be to spend it. When we have extra money, most of us also have a list of wants in our heads: "If I had a few hundred dollars, I'd buy a piece of bedroom furniture, take the family on a trip, and buy that new gas-powered lawnmower." But stop for a moment and think about the options. After you've paid off your major debts, this extra cash is money that you can save. Put it in your 401(k), establish an emergency fund, invest for college and retirement. To keep impulses in check, put the money out of reach as soon as you receive it—or better yet, have it deducted from your paycheck.

Saving for the Short Term

To ensure that you can access your cash when you need it in a hurry, you may want to put some of it in risk-free or low-risk, liquid investments such as savings accounts, certificates of deposit (CDs), money market mutual funds, Treasury bills, or stable bonds and equity funds—conservative, safe investments that have fairly paltry and fixed returns.

A typical fixed-income, liquid investment is a CD. This can be a good place to start. A $500 investment will grow to $642 before taxes after ten years if you put it in a savings account that averages 2.5 percent interest, or to $823 if you put it into a CD with a 5 percent yield. The same investment will grow to $1,354 if you put it into stocks with an average annual rate of return of 10 percent, but what you gain in income you will lose in liquidity and safety of your principal.

Saving for Education

Before you begin to estimate how much to save for your children's education, answer a couple of questions: What percentage of your children's college expenses will you pay for? How much will college cost when it's time for your children to begin attending? The answers to these two questions will enable you to establish an education savings goal and to determine how much you need to save each month to reach that goal.

The key to saving for education is to start early and be consistent. Put money into the college fund monthly, and let compounding do the work.

You can set aside funds to save for college in several ways. It's a good idea to get into the habit of saving funds monthly.

One common savings vehicle that's safe, because it's federally insured, is a savings account. However, the interest paid is low. On the plus side, money in a savings account is easy to get to if you need cash.

One step above this is an insured money market account or a CD. The interest rates are a bit higher than a regular savings account, depending on the amount of money you put into it. This is a wonderful way to start to save to move up to a bit riskier investment.

If you have between $500 and $1,000, you can buy a mutual fund. There are different types, including government-guaranteed ones that invest in Treasury bills, notes, or bonds. A bill matures in less than 1 year. A note is issued between 1 and 5 years. A bond is issued for 5 to 30 years. The interest rates are better the longer you invest. This is also a safe investment because it's government-backed. However, the fund rates aren't much better than the interest rates paid on a money market or CD.

The best way to invest for college to get the best return that offers more risk but greater rewards is for you to consider a mutual fund that invests in blue chip or aggressive growth stocks, such as small cap companies that hope to become large companies someday, or foreign securities. When you invest in these funds, your money is pooled with funds of other investors. A professional fund manager invests the pool of money. For the past ten years, many of these funds have had returns of about 14 percent.

Another option is to set up a portfolio builder or a dollar cost average account to save for college. You start the account with as little as $500 and add a minimum of $25 or more each month. Again, the money is put in a pool and invested in a fund. The compounding effect is astronomical.

What about taxes on these debt and equity investments? The Uniform Gift to Minors Act allows you to invest the money in your child's name and Social Security number with you as custodian until he or she is 18. Your child will be taxed on the interest at the lower tax rate. If your child earns less than $1,000 in interest in any given year, he won't have to pay taxes. If you've put in $5,000 in your child's name and the fund earns 12 percent, you can earn $600 in one year.

Individual retirement accounts (IRAs) for education are also a safe and effective way to compound money. These are administered by financial institutions such as banks.

The Roth IRA dictates that if you have $2,000 of earned income, you can add $2,000 to a Roth IRA, assuming your and your husband's joint adjusted gross income doesn't exceed $160,000. If single, your income can be no more than $95,000, also adjusted gross income. The money placed in the Roth IRA earns interest that is automatically added to the initial account. Everything it earns up to the time you pull it out is tax free.

An education IRA is another tool that is designed to generate money for your child's education. You can make an after-tax contribution to the IRA of $500 to each child under 18 years of age. You can self-direct the IRA into mutual funds or individual stocks. If you have $500 you've put into this IRA and it earns 20 percent in a mutual fund, it will be worth $600 one year later. The earnings go right back in and begin to compound. Any money accrued is tax free for your child's education. All funds must be withdrawn by the time your child reaches age 30.

To glean more information about saving for your child's higher education, consult your banker or a financial advisor. Information on educational savings is also available on the Internet and in libraries and bookstores.

Saving for Retirement

How much money will you need to retire at your current standard of living? Most financial experts say you'll need at least 80 percent of your current income to live on. When you retire, chances are you won't have a mortgage anymore, and your transportation and clothing expenses will probably decrease. On the other hand, you will spend more on medical care as you age.

You should define your retirement goals sooner rather than later. Determine how much money you will need to live on, figure out how much income you can expect, develop a savings and investment strategy, then monitor it and make adjustments as needed. Also, ask yourself when you want to retire, what standard of living you desire during retirement, what you want to do in your retirement years, where you'll live after you retire, and whether you'll have any dependents during your retirement.

Assume that you will have some type of retirement income such as your 401(k), government benefits, yes, Social Security (which still increases every year but doesn't rise enough because it is pegged to a price index that doesn't keep up with inflation, known as CPI-W), your savings and investments, employer-sponsored pension and savings, employer-sponsored retiree health, annuities, and IRAs.

Your Annual Expenses

	Now	After Retirement

HOUSING EXPENSES
  Rent or mortgage
  Property taxes
  Heat
  Electricity
  Property insurance

LIVING EXPENSES
  Telephone
  Television
  Food
  Clothing
  Laundry/dry cleaning
  Car maintenance and depreciation
  Traveling to work
  Insurance premiums
  Company pension contributions
  Medical insurance
  Disability insurance
  Car insurance/expenses
  Medical/dental bills
  Extras
    Restaurants
    Entertainment
    Hobbies
    Recreation
    Travel
    Gifts
    Magazines, books, newspapers
    Pocket money
  Miscellaneous

TOTAL ANNUAL EXPENSES

Retirement Planning

If your company offers a 401(k) plan, take full advantage. The company may be increasing your investment by 25, 50, or even 100 percent by matching it with its own dollars. Essentially this is free money. When you invest in the 401(k), most companies offer multiple investment options. Tilt your 401(k) investment choices toward equities such as stocks, depending on your risk tolerance, age, and allocation of your other investments. It's best to have a mix. Diversification may protect you from ups and downs in a particular asset category or industry. If you have 10 or more years before you retire, keep no more than 10 to 25 percent of your 401(k) in company stock.

There are expenditures to consider as well. Don't forget that whatever retirement income you receive, it gets taxed. In addition, property taxes may still rise, as do the taxes on your Social Security benefits. Don't ignore that bugaboo known as inflation, which can cut into the value of your annuity or pension. Also, you may have more medical and prescription drug expenses as you age, and it's likely the price of both will rise. Don't forget you'll have to pay taxes when you pull money out of your retirement accounts or sell stocks and mutual funds with capital gains.

There are several sites on the Internet where you can find answers to your questions about joining or borrowing from a 401(k) plan:

Quicken.com
<www.quicken.com/retirement/
  401k>

The 401(k) Company
<www.the401k.com/faq.html>

401Kafé
<www.401kafe.com>

401k Center for Employers
<401kcenter.com>

PAI Pension Services
<www.paipension.com/
  info401.htm>

Estate Planning

Okay. You've gone through the paces of learning how to budget, and you're on your feet financially. You've experienced all the pleasant and unpleasant surprises. In addition to learning how to hone your spending habits, you can also enhance your financial profile for the future.

One way to do this is through estate planning, that is, arranging your personal affairs now so that they are in order in case of death or mental incapacity. When you do the planning yourself ahead of time, you ensure that it's done according to your wishes and that there will be enough to cover debts and expenses such as personal loans, taxes, bills, and mortgage payments. Estate planning involves preparing a will, tax planning, signing a power of attorney, and purchasing life insurance. Consult a lawyer to assist you, and make sure you have an up-to-date will, because your will sets the parameters for distribution of your estate.

Ways to Earn Money

1. Increase your income by taking a part-time job and save the second income.

2. Don't leave funds in a passbook savings account. Switch funds into money market accounts and other vehicles with a higher return.

3. Don't miss out on a 401(k) plan that matches your contribution. Contribute the highest amount you can afford so that you can get the free money.

4. Get professional money management for free by investing in a mutual fund.

Ways to Save Money

1. Don't buy on impulse. Research anything before you buy, particularly big-ticket items. It will slow down your purchasing.

2. Comparison shop.

3. Take lunch and snacks to work so you can avoid expensive lunches out and vending machines. But once a week or so do go out for lunch with colleagues, networking is important.

4. If you smoke, quit for your health and your bottom line.

5. Rather than taking on major remodeling projects, transform the space you have with cosmetic changes such as paint, paper, and new knobs. Keep walls, plumbing, and heating fixtures where they are.

6. Extend the life of your appliances and systems by maintaining them carefully—on a semiannual or annual basis, or whatever is recommended by professionals.

7. Limit yourself to one credit card, and don't carry high-interest balances on it. Negotiate your rate telling the credit card firm that you'll transfer your balance to another card unless it gives you a lower rate.

8. Avoid paying expensive bank fees. Don't use another bank's cash machine; don't bounce checks; don't incur fees for low balances. Call the bank and complain if you're being nickeled and dimed. It's bad enough that savings rates are at subinflation levels and now banks hike charges on everything from savings accounts to bounced checks.

9. Don't buy insurance that you don't need. You need conventional life insurance if you have dependents and are a wage earner, and you also need homeowners' coverage. You don't need credit card insurance, dread-disease insurance, or accidental death insurance such as flight insurance.

Ways to Save Money
(continued)

10. Don't pay too much property tax. Check your assessment at the local assessor's office. Make sure the number of bedrooms or the square footage of your home isn't
exaggerated in the assessment. Then, compare your assessment with those of at least three comparable homes
on your block. If your home appears to be overvalued,
have it reassessed. Don't forget that when you remodel
your home, your annual property taxes increase.

Ways to Earn Extra Money

1. Turn your hobby into a business. Restore furniture,
   repair home appliances, or take in sewing. Advertise in
   local newspapers and on the radio. If your skills are
   rusty, take courses at a community college or trade school.

2. Do temp work that can lead to a permanent job.

3. Convert items you no longer use into money. Sell your
   old computer equipment or turn it into a tax write-off
   by donating it to a nonprofit organization.

4. Reduce cleaning bills by buying only machine-washable
   clothes.

5. Frequent discount clothing shops.

6. Clip coupons and watch for sale items at the grocery store.

7. Instead of buying extended service contracts on your office equipment and appliances, self-insure. Put the cost
   of the contract into a money market account and you
   may save more than enough to cover repairs and replace the equipment when the time comes.

8. Cut long distance costs by choosing the right carrier.

It's best to have a good relationship with a financial professional who can advise you on an ongoing basis. You don't have to be an expert yourself, but you should depend on someone who is.

Preventing Foreclosure

The word "foreclosure" can be scary. Foreclosure happens when your lender takes over or repossesses your home because you have defaulted on your mortgage. When this happens, you have to move out. Losing your home in this manner will kill your credit rating and seriously impair your ability to get any type of loan in the future. And if your home is worth less than the amount you still owe on your mortgage at the time of foreclosure, you could be in even deeper financial straits. Avoid foreclosure at all costs.

If you think you may be headed in the direction of a foreclosure, it's time to take action. This requires a bit of courage on your part. You have to contact your lender and work out a deal. The worst thing you can do is evade the issue. Diminish your risk by nipping the situation in the bud. If you stick your head in the sand because you're so anxious about your inability to pay, you may lose your home.

Your lender will most likely work with you. Provide her with all of your financial information, and she can help draft a plan.

You and your lender have several options:

Special forbearance. The lender may work out a plan to waive payments for a period of time or readjust your payment schedule.

Mortgage modification. You may be able to refinance the debt or extend the terms of the mortgage so your payments will be smaller and more affordable.

Partial claim. If your loan is between 4 and 12 months overdue, if you are not yet in foreclosure, and if you are able to start making full payments, your lender may be able to procure a partial interest-free loan from the Department of Housing and Urban Development (HUD). When HUD extends you this type of loan, your lender pays the amount you owe, you execute a promissory note, and a lien is placed on your property until the interest-free promissory note is paid in full.

Pre-foreclosure sale. If you sell the property before foreclosure, you can avoid having a foreclosure on your credit report. There are conditions to doing this, however: the appraised value must be at least 70 percent of the amount you owe, the sale price must be at least 95 percent of the appraised value; you must be at least two months behind in paying your mortgage; and you must sell in three to five months.

Deed in lieu of foreclosure. Another way to save face is the deed-in-lieu-of-foreclosure benefit. You essentially make a trade with the mortgage company. You give back your property to the lender and your credit remains intact. This option works best if you cannot benefit from other options, if you cannot sell your house, and if you don't have any other mortgages in default.

Bankruptcy. As a last resort, discuss with your attorney the possibility of recasting of the debt to stop the foreclosure, or declaring a Chapter 13 bankruptcy.

Chapter 13 not only stops the foreclosure, but it forces the lender to take the delinquent amount of payment and amend the debt. If your house payments are $400 a month and you're six months behind, you now owe $2,400 plus attorneys fees, which can average more than $1,000, bringing your tab to $3,400. When you file the Chapter 13, you work out a payment schedule according to which you pay the money back over a certain amount of time at perhaps an affordable $100 a month for 36 months. You can get another job raking leaves to augment your income.

This way you won't lose your house. Chapter 13 will also prevent your wages from being garnished and your car from being repossessed. Of course, bankruptcy will appear on your credit rating.

When you fear foreclosure, you are in a very vulnerable position, so you must be especially vigilant about avoiding scams like equity skimming: A buyer says he'll pay off your mortgage and give you money after your house is sold. He may tell you to move out and may rent the house to someone else, but he doesn't pay off the mortgage. Instead, he allows the home to go into foreclosure. If you have legal representation, you will be less likely to fall prey to scam artists.

What will you face if, despite all your best efforts, foreclosure appears to be inevitable?

Although each case is different, foreclosures follow a fairly standard process. If you miss a number of payments or violate a condition of your mortgage agreement, you will be on the wanted list of your lender and possibly of HUD for a deficiency judgment. The lender may threaten to foreclose your mortgage and put your home up for sale. You will be notified by certified mail a certain number of days before the sale date. Most lenders will accept reinstatement at that point if you agree to pay the mortgage and other fees incurred.

If an agreement is not reached, the lender may then advertise your home for a period of roughly 30 days in a general-circulation newspaper. Once your property is sold, the lender keeps the amount owed. If foreclosure occurs, you are obligated to pay off your first mortgage, and you may be liable to pay off a second mortgage, if you have one.

If you are threatened with foreclosure, you should hire a lawyer. The lawyer will protect you from signing the wrong papers, make sure you get everything in writing, and help keep you from digging yourself into an even deeper hole.

Monthly Expenses

Fixed Expenses

Mortgage	$_____
Utilities (give an average if not on a monthly budget plan)	
Electricity	_____
Gas	_____
Heat	_____
Water	_____
Day care services	_____
Cable TV/special channels	_____
Service contracts	_____
Regular savings	_____
Holiday/Christmas fund	_____
Car loan payments	_____
Other loan/debt payments	_____
	_____
	_____
	_____
Alimony	_____
Child support	_____
Other	
_____	_____
_____	_____
_____	_____

Irregular Expenses (Divide annual expenses by 12 to find average monthly expenses.)

Taxes	
Federal income tax	$_____
State income tax	_____
Property tax (if not part of mortgage)	_____

(continued)

Monthly Expenses
(continued)

Other

_____   _____
_____   _____
_____   _____

Insurance Premiums $_____
   Homeowners   _____
   Auto
   Life   _____
   Medical   _____
   Disability   _____
   Other

_____   _____
_____   _____
_____   _____

Car registration   _____
Driver's license fees   _____

Variable Expenses (Divide annual expenses
by 12 to find average monthly expenses.)
Car maintenance and repairs $_____
Gas/oil   _____
Parking   _____
Public transportation/taxis   _____
Dining out   _____
Groceries   _____
Dry cleaning   _____
Clothing   _____
Baby-sitting services   _____

Monthly Expenses
(continued)

Home maintenance/repairs	_____
Telephone (including cellular and long distance)	_____
Furniture/home furnishings	_____
Doctor visits/prescriptions	_____
Dental	_____
Newspapers, magazines, books, videos	_____
Alcoholic beverages	_____
Movies, concerts, plays, etc.	_____
Health club membership	_____
Other memberships	
_____	_____
_____	_____
_____	_____
Veterinary bills	_____
Pet food	_____
Personal care items	_____
Hairdressing	_____
Charitable donations	_____
Gifts	_____
Vacations	_____
Spending money/lunch money	_____
Miscellaneous	_____
Total monthly expenses	$_____
Total monthly income	$_____
Less total monthly expenses	_____
Cash Remaining	$_____

Assets

Checking account(s)	$_____
Savings account(s)	_____
Value of home	_____
Value of automobiles	_____
Cash value of life insurance	_____
Term deposits/CDs	_____
Stocks, bonds	_____
Mutual funds	_____
Pension holdings/401(k)	_____
Total assets	$_____

Liabilities

Mortgage (balance outstanding)	$_____
Income/property taxes	_____
Car loan (balance outstanding)	_____
Credit cards (balance outstanding)	_____
Personal line of credit (balance outstanding)	_____
Other loans (balance outstanding)	_____
Unpaid bills	_____
Other obligations	
_____	_____
_____	_____
_____	_____
Total liabilities	$_____

Your Gross Monthly Income

	Average Monthly Amount
Gross pay (before taxes and other deductions)	$_____
Overtime and part-time pay, commissions	_____
Tips/bonuses	_____
Business or investment earnings	_____
Dividends/interest earnings	_____
Pension/Social Security benefits	_____
Veterans Administration benefits	_____
Unemployment compensation	_____
Disability	_____
Public assistance	_____
Alimony/child support	_____
Other	
_____	_____
_____	_____
_____	_____
Total gross monthly income	$_____

Monthly Budget Worksheet

Net Monthly Income

Total gross monthly income	$_____
Minus payroll deductions	_____
Total net monthly income	$_____

Monthly Expenses/Savings

Current housing expenses	$_____
Monthly mortgage payment	_____
Property taxes and insurance	
(if not included in mortgage payment)	_____
Average monthly utilities	_____
Allowance for maintenance expenses	_____
Nonhousing expenses	_____
Savings (emergency fund)	_____
Total monthly expenses and savings	$_____

Remaining Discretionary Income

Total net monthly income	$_____
Minus total monthly expenses and savings	_____
Funds available for short- and long-term investments	$_____

Investment Goals	Total Amount Needed	Monthly Savings
Short-Term Goals		
1. _____	_____	_____
2. _____	_____	_____
3. _____	_____	_____
Long-Term Goals		
1. _____	_____	_____
2. _____	_____	_____
3. _____	_____	_____

CHAPTER 5

Put a Little Pizzazz in Your Life, or 118 Ideas for Personalizing Your Home

You might think that once you move into your home and start to unpack all your belongings, you'll be home free. Unfortunately, you won't be. Figuring out where to put your furniture, where to hang family photos, and how to arrange all your knick-knacks takes a lot of thought, time, and hard work.

And that's just the tip of the iceberg. When you finally sit down to enjoy your new surroundings, you will start to see all the warts—all the things in your home you'd like to improve. You may not like the white walls in your living room, so you think about painting them. The hardwood floors in the dining room may need to be refinished because they are scratched and too dark for your light-colored furnishings. The molding in the kitchen may need a new coat of paint. You also recognize that you have a lot of empty corners and blank walls. So you try to look beyond the obvious and imagine the possibilities. You envision turning your ugly duckling into a gorgeous swan.

But there's that little problem called money. Few of us can afford to buy a home and instantly decorate it so it looks exactly the way we want. As the ideas for how to decorate and arrange furniture start accumulating in your mind, the dollars are adding up. But here's where reason must supercede fantasy. You need to decide how and if you can afford to make cosmetic changes.

If you can't afford to make changes yet, don't despair. There are ways to give your new place a lived-in, loved look without running up exorbitant credit card balances that you can't afford to pay.

First of all, no house ever really starts from scratch. Whether you're beginning with family hand-me-downs or furnishings from your previous apartment, you usually have some kind of a core to work around. So you begin to fill in. You don't need to go for a particular "look," especially if you already own pieces that aren't of the same style or period. What you need to do is project your own sense of style, which you can discover by looking through books and home magazines, walking through model homes and furniture departments, and analyzing the things you already have and love.

Remember the virtues of simplicity, efficiency, honesty, and charm. What's practical can be beautiful and can span all budgets. Real style, say some experts, can cost next to nothing. Giving your home a personality that reflects who you and other family members are can be remarkably inexpensive if you take the time and don't expect an instant, magazine-like decor.

You give your home personality by making the right choices and buying quality when you can because good things last. Filling in where you can afford to is fine. You can take advantage of the new thrift-store-chic look, recycling someone else's discarded belongings, which may be in excellent condition.

Getting Started

Exactly where do you begin? First, make a list of every improvement you want to make in your home both in the immediate future and over the long range. Save the list on paper or in a computer file so you can check it periodically. Decide what you can do yourself, what you'll need to hire someone for, what proj-

Decorating Truisms

- Any color you like is never out of style.

- Vinyl is a terrific practical and inexpensive floor covering for children's rooms, bathrooms, and kitchens.

- Rooms should never be overlighted; it's not good for the eyes and it's not good for the pocketbook.

- Windows can be left bare so you can enjoy outdoor views and create a stark, dramatic effect.

- Upholstered furniture can be covered in a neutral fabric, and you can use slipcovers to change its color along with the seasons or your mood.

- Yard sale finds can be painted or reupholstered. When different periods are mixed together, the eclecticism adds instant panache to any home.

- Good hardware gives a room a sense of quality and permanence, even if it doesn't match or isn't from the same period.

- No room has ambiance unless it is used and lived in.

- A house shouldn't look like a model from a magazine; nobody really lives in perfect settings anyway.

ects you can avoid until you've saved more money, and what single project would be a wish come true. Following are 118 ideas divided into those four categories.

Do-It-Yourself Projects

Even if you're not terribly handy or creative, there are numerous inexpensive projects that you can do on your own to personalize your house.

Painting is one of the easiest and least expensive ways to change the look of a room. You visit the paint store and stand before a rack of paint samples, riffling through the blues. Somewhere among the color samples lies just the shade you crave for your bedroom. You wonder if you could mix it yourself. If you don't go ahead and paint now, you'll end up living with plain white walls chosen not by desire, but by default. (Of course, many people love white; if it's what you choose, go ahead and take chances with it.)

If you're uncertain about what color you want, become a color collector. Try out your samples on the paint store's color-matching computer. Try the color on one wall of a room and live with it for awhile. You can always cover it with another color if you decide it's not right for you.

If you're painting the room yourself, remember that a paint job is only as good as the prep work that comes first. You must be sure you do the following before you paint:

- Be sure that you have plenty of primer, paint, brushes, rollers, and drop cloths.
- Clean walls with soap and water.
- Patch holes and cracks with spackling putty, then sand them well.
- Scrape off peeling paint, sand the edges of the scraped area, spackle any accidental gouges, then sand again.
- Roll on one or two coats of primer.
- Cover remaining flaws with spackling putty, then sand.
- Prime again.

Now you're ready to paint.

1. White makes a room look larger, and colors look clearer against it. For the trim, walls, and ceiling, you can use three distinct shades of white if you like.
2. To keep a room looking soft, paint the trim and ceiling white and the walls a medium gray. As a matter of fact,

it's usually a good idea to paint the ceiling a lighter color than the walls.

3. How about a wash of color? Use a latex, water-based paint that is easier to apply and clean up, dries faster, has a more pleasant odor, and doesn't yellow.

4. In bathrooms and kitchens, where your mother always swore by oil-based paint, how about a water-based acrylic or hard-drying latex epoxy enamel?

5. Paint a room or two a zany color such as deep violet. Cover dated paneling with sunny, flat colors to create a new look for your room. Paneling provides texture for a painted surface.

6. Splatter paint on an old floor. Invite your children to participate. Turn on the music, wear old clothes, and you'll have an instant work of family performance art.

7. Put a wallpaper border around the perimeter of a room near the ceiling. It's easier than wallpapering an entire room, and it adds a distinctive flavor. Prepasted wallpaper borders are very easy to hang.

8. Paint or stencil an area rug on the floorboards with diluted latex paint. Seal with polyurethane.

9. Instead of replacing a cracked plaster ceiling, patch it up and cover it with wallpaper.

10. Before installing a new floor, check out the original floorboards that are hidden under peeling linoleum.

11. Make your home shine. If your new house was previously owned, give it a top to bottom cleaning and scrubbing. Clean grills, vents, moldings, and baseboards. Before you hang them, clean your curtains and blinds.

12. Buy a birdhouse and hang it in a tree; chirping birds will definitely make you feel you're not alone in your new abode and neighborhood. Once a few birds start coming, buy another birdhouse and you'll begin to draw a flock.

13. Line all your cabinets and shelves in your bathroom and kitchen with pretty shelf paper that has a pattern

that reflects something about you and other members of your family.

14. Buy a new mailbox.

15. Buy new doormats for all the doors.

16. Plant a few new flowering shrubs. If it's fall, plant a lot of bulbs that will come up in spring and throughout the following summer. Choose an array of colors that look nice with the color of your front door and shutters. Ask for help when you make selections at your favorite garden store.

17. Put pretty scented colored bars of soap and some potpourri in all the bathrooms of the house, not just the one used by guests. Place them in attractive ceramic bowls or dishes you found at a garage sale. Occasionally add a vase with some fresh or dried flowers.

18. Keep a flowering plant in your kitchen or front hall so the fragrance permeates the air.

19. Buy some small pots of herbs to grow in your kitchen or another well-lighted area. They have a nice fragrance and will enhance your cooking.

20. Old bowls, small to gigantic, make handsome containers for all kinds of objects, from seashells to kindling, and add interest when placed under tables.

21. Invite friends or family for dinner or a party. Your house will immediately seem move alive when you entertain and use all your best dishes, glassware, and silver. If you're nervous about cooking, ask each guest to bring a dish, or buy part of the meal in the prepared-food section of your favorite grocery store.

22. Once a month, rearrange the magazines and collectibles on your coffee table and side tables so your living room doesn't feel like a museum where nobody sits, reads, watches TV, or talks to one another. One sure-fire way to get people to use the room is to bring out some board games and have the entire family play chess, checkers, or Scrabble. Pop some popcorn and you're all set.

23. Install a bulletin board or chalkboard in the kitchen or breakfast room so you have a place to write messages, announce the dinner menu, or simply share fun jokes or riddles.

24. Buying new hangers will inspire you to organize your clothing neatly. For your guest closet, you might crochet covers for the hangers to make them special.

25. Buy at least one pretty new pot to leave out in your kitchen, particularly if you've had your old pots and pans for years.

26. Frame and hang some of the photos that are now packed into boxes, which isn't good for the photographs or for keeping happy memories alive. Copy your originals at a photo shop and frame the copies. Keep originals in photo albums to preserve them. Do a rogue's gallery of pictures on the wall leading up the stairs. Glass prevents photos from fading. Don't allow a wood frame to make direct contact with a photograph. The acids in the wood will stain the photo.

27. Buy new spices and arrange them alphabetically in a drawer or cabinet. Buy a few new ones you've never tried and find recipes to use them in.

28. Save up for a nice stereo system and every few months let a different member of your family buy a new CD.

29. Change the knobs on cabinets you can't afford to replace and you'll have an instant new look. Also, if you don't like the color of the cabinets, spray paint them a new color.

30. Put decorative candles in your bathrooms.

31. Put up a hammock between two large trees.

32. Get a big stack of logs for your fireplace, and bring out the skewers, marshmallows, graham crackers, and chocolate and have s'mores in your house when it's freezing outdoors. Make some hot chocolate and look at old family photos together. You can even roast chestnuts, like the song says.

33. Go to a garage or estate sale and buy some inexpensive items for your mantle such as old candlesticks, tiny picture frames, or little toys to line up in a row. Previously owned items do show wear and tear, but superficial imperfections do not hinder an object's purpose, and that look of age, known as patina, is something that money can't buy.

34. Look for old linens. Dig deep into boxes of musty old linens at estate sales and you may be rewarded with hand-embroidered dish towels that you can use in the guest bathroom or at your dinner tables as fancy napkins. One woman took red, white, and blue towels and tablecloths and turned them into a colorful, multi-patterned sofa cover. Old linens can be machine washed on gentle with detergent. To keep fine linens in good shape, wash them in cold water on the gentle cycle, then run the final rinse cycle twice, tossing in a few tablespoons of white vinegar to neutralize any soap residue. Let them air dry. Store them by wrapping them in white cotton towels or blankets to prevent them from coming into direct contact with wood, which can discolor them.

35. Tack up a strip of decorative molding on the walls of a plain room for a homier look.

36. Collectibles make more of a statement when they're grouped together. For example, Spode china and eye-catching mercury glass work well together in a kitchen. Start a collection and group the items together on a table—snowglobes, decoys, teacups, or miniature pitchers. If possible, use one of the items to hold flowers. In any display, try balancing tall objects with short, chunky ones.

37. Replace the old pillows on some of your sofas or beds with new ones in vivid accent colors. Keep room schemes fresh by moving pillows. If colors flow from room to room, so will your patterns.

38. Add texture to a room by displaying your handiwork, using needlepoint for pillows or knitting for an afghan.

39. Subscribe to a home furnishings magazine that will give you loads of new decorating ideas. Or if you don't want to subscribe, go to your public library and take out a stack of books and recent magazines.
40. Install decorative lighting outside—in the trees or along a walkway. It will look pretty at night and make you feel safer when coming home.
41. Buy a book about feng shui, the Chinese practice of structuring places in an auspicious manner, and follow some of the ideas. Some say it will bring you harmony, peace, and good luck.
42. Place an attractive box or rack for outgoing mail on a table near the front door.
43. Create an air of welcome by hanging a wreath on the front door or placing a topiary tree on either side of your doorway.
44. Use copper tubing as a curtain rod or cooper pipe as a wonderful alternative to a wooden stair rail. Industrial materials can be very inexpensive and are often found at estate sales.
45. Plant an indoor window box to bring blooming color into your home.
46. Buy a table and chairs at your nearest import store, where you can find good design at a good price. Or pull vintage, French, iron, or garden chairs up to a home-made table built from plywood and skirted in cleanable cotton fabric.
47. Rearrange seating pieces to make the room look different.
48. Build a divider screen. Old shutters hinged together make an excellent screen or room divider.
49. Give a quick lift to tired window treatments by using tiebacks. Find small, lightweight items like plastic pears, grapes, oranges, or other shapes at a craft store and glue them to a strip of material to serve as a tieback. You can also try colorful sponge cutouts, buttons, hair bows, barrettes, sea shells, charms, pins, antique brooches, political buttons, or tie tacks.

50. Chairs and tables don't have to match, and even the chairs themselves can be from different periods and in different colors. Banister-back chairs that need a coat of paint will mix easily with the wooden dining table. Put a bedroom bureau in the dining room for storage instead of a traditional buffet. An old gate-leg table can take the place of a big buffet or china cabinet, displaying dinnerware that's too pretty to hide.

51. Hang family mementos above the fireplace. Display the photos with large white mats around a big mirror. Lots of small doodads for the mantle and a few bold baskets and bowls for the hearth complete the arrangement.

52. Fill the space under a high window with a leggy sofa table and old metal baskets, which are a good place to stash odds and ends.

53. Have your furniture play multiple roles. A Parson's table can serve as a spot for bill paying, reading, or garden planning, and with a quick change, it can be a dining table or a desk for your home office.

54. Set up a kitchen work center that is situated out of the main traffic flow as a mini home office.

55. Use sun-resistant fabrics as window coverings so they won't have to be replaced for years. Acrylic is the best for sun resistance, and it's affordable. Polyester comes in a close second place. Cotton, rayon, and acetate are moderately resistant. Nylon and silk offer poor sun resistance, but if lined, they will resist the sun's rays longer.

56. In a bedroom, use recycled material such as a section of picket fence for a headboard.

57. When mixing pillows of different fabrics, vary the sizes and shapes.

58. Edit your belongings. Remember, the less clutter you have, the more noticeable individual items are and the fresher the room becomes.

59. Use fabric with a vivid hue to cover the seat of one chair. It will draw eclectic objects together while jazzing up the room.

60. Bring style to dated furniture or to a storage sore spot by sewing a clever cover up. Skirt an old sofa table, a stereo stand, back-to-back file cabinets, or even a short bookcase.
61. Use two crisscrossing runners to make a tablecloth that protects a treasured table but doesn't cover it completely.
62. Warm a window with a snug quilt or a rag-rug shade. In summer, hang a curtain made of flower sheets over the window for light control. In autumn, add the cozy texture of a soft blanket draped swag style over a decorative wooden pole.
63. Work with other family members to begin finishing your basement.
64. Affordably remodel your kitchen by replacing a countertop or changing the knobs on drawers.

 Remodeling Your Kitchen for Less

Whether you're gutting your kitchen and starting over, or just adding a bit of visual vigor, kitchen renewal can be pricey. Here are some ideas to help you put your best frugal foot forward:

- Take stock. Assess the current situation. Are you decorating around a refrigerator that needs to be replaced next year? Do you really need new cabinets, or would replacing just the doors solve the problem?

- Establish a budget.

- Do your homework. Clip ideas from magazines, read consumer publications that rate appliances and building materials, and get design books from the library before you buy. Always comparison shop.

(continued)

Remodeling Your Kitchen for Less
(continued)

- Work with people who share your sentiments about value, quality, and thrift. You don't want someone to pressure you into buying something you really can't afford.

- Never buy on impulse. Design first, buy later.

- If the kitchen is starting out in pretty good shape, work with it. Bleach a dark oak floor; paint walls and trim white. Don't hesitate to paint dark-stained cabinets. There are many paints that cover wood completely.

- Appliances can be refinished, giving an old range, refrigerator, and dishwasher a face lift. You can also reglaze porcelain tubs and sinks yourself.

- Vinyl tile or sheet tile can be painted if you don't want to replace it. An exterior deck paint or even an interior latex applied with brush and roller and topped with two or three coats of polyurethane sealer will put a brand-new floor underfoot.

- Cover old surfaces. Install new underlayment and vinyl tiles over an aging floor, nail painted sheet paneling over dated wallpaper and backsplashes, and lay ceramic tiles over old laminate countertops.

- Use trivets that mimic hand-painted tile, nailing them up as a quick backsplash.

- Stencil flowers around an arched doorway to call attention to the architecture.

- Change the lighting. Buy halogen floor lamps that bounce light off the ceiling and install them yourself.

- Install decorative moldings in the kitchen, such as crown moldings at the ceiling and a chair rail on the walls. Consider replacing trim around existing windows and doors to give the kitchen shape and detail.

Remodeling Your Kitchen for Less
(continued)

- Install a jazzy new faucet set on an existing sink (copper faucets last the longest); buy new curtains, blinds, or shutters; put a new tablecloth on the breakfast table and new seat cushions on the chairs and stools; purchase new dish towels and pot holders; and place new artwork and decorative accessories throughout the room.

- Reface cabinet drawers and frames with new laminate.

- Upgrade countertops. If they are laminate, have the edges bullnosed or add a wood strip for an interesting look. Or change your countertops altogether. It's less expensive than redoing the whole kitchen or bathroom, and it will give the room an instant new look. Choose a neutral color that will work with your current appliances and that a future owner will also be likely to find appealing. Laminate countertops are reasonably priced, but some solid surfaces or Corian knock-offs such as Swanstone are also affordable. Any kitchen contractor can advise you and do the work.

- If you hire someone to redo your kitchen, do the demolition yourself to save money. Before you take sledgehammers to a wall, however, make sure it's not a load-bearing wall. And assume there are electrical wires and pipes in the wall. Damaging them might disrupt your burglar alarm, phone, or plumbing. If you have a home demolition party, make sure your homeowners insurance provides coverage for on-the-job injuries to your volunteers.

- Look for recycled cabinets, if you want to replace your old ones. Call local cabinet dealers, contractors, friends, relatives, and neighbors. Not all cabinets have to have started as cabinets, and they don't have to match one another. People are also doing mix and match countertops.

(continued)

Remodeling Your Kitchen for Less
(continued)

Shop architectural salvage yards, antique stores, local flea markets. If you're looking for excellent finds, arrive early and stand in line at the entrance. Be thorough; look through everything, including items stashed under tables. Be decisive when you spot something you want. If it's within your budget, grab it.

- Again, be creative with furniture pieces. An old bookcase can work as a pantry cabinet. An antique library table can make a charming island in your kitchen.

- Separate cooktops and ovens are expensive to buy and install and take up more space, so it's best to stick to a one-piece unit if you can.

- If a built-in refrigerator is beyond your means, buy a less expensive, free-standing model and give it a built-in look. Build an alcove for it out of drywall, or surround it with tall, pantry-style cabinets.

- Don't buy appliances with all the bells and whistles, but be sure when you do buy that you compare the annual energy-consumption ratings of various models. You may have to pay slightly more up front for efficiency that will save you money down the road.

Projects That You May Need to Hire Someone For

No matter how many books and magazines you read and how many how-to television shows you watch, you still may not get the hang of being Mr. or Ms. Fix-It. Even if it's driving everyone in the house crazy and you have become the family joke because you break everything you try to fix, it's okay. Not everybody can tackle every homeowner task.

You can periodically hire someone. When you do, just be sure to get a recommendation and a firm estimate (preferably in writing), and don't pay the full amount until you're satisfied. As a rule, if you have to choose between expensive labor and expensive materials, go for the labor. Professionals can save you money by taking that risk out of what you do. Good tradespeople can help you keep material costs down while giving you a highly individualized custom look. Think about what work you are willing and able to do. You may tackle demolition, but it takes a great deal more skill to put a kitchen together.

65. Organize your closets.
66. Organize your desk. Get rid of excess books and odds and ends.
67. Have a good electrician evaluate your lighting outside and in each of your rooms. Prioritize what needs to be done, and have the electrician come back and work every six months until you get all the work done. If an electrician is not in the budget, ask at your home center about electrical kits you can use to install lighting yourself—external ground lighting behind shrubs, for example.
68. Buy an unpainted piece of furniture, stain or paint it a favorite color, and use it for excess odds and ends.
69. Install an exhaust fan in your attic if your house doesn't have one. It will help to cool the house on hot days, cutting down on your air-conditioning bills and protecting your furnishings by keeping the temperature in your home cooler.
70. Add indoor window shutters in one or two rooms; they are less expensive than many window treatments and appeal to owners of both contemporary and traditional homes. You can paint or stain the shutters and install them yourself.

71. Remove old and dirty wall-to-wall carpeting and replace it with hardwood floors, which offer a good return on your investment because they appeal to prospective buyers. The floors should be installed professionally, but you can tear up the old carpeting yourself.

72. Beef up your bathroom. Build a broad ledge over your vanity for toiletries. If you have shallow drawers, buy plastic organizers. Install built-ins at the end of walls that stretch floor to ceiling, with each compartment hiding behind laminate-faced bifold doors.

73. Clean your gutters in the fall and spring or hire someone to do it. It will help prevent leaks when the weather turns bad. Paint your gutters if they need it to spiff up the front of your house. You might also add a coat of paint to trim and shutters.

74. Install a fireplace in your family room or living room. The premade firebox type doesn't require brickwork or digging. The prefabricated chase, made of siding, cedar, or aluminum, is nailed to the house. A fireplace is a wonderful focal point for a room and also helps heat your home in winter.

75. If you're artistic, do your own flower arranging. Many party stores have accessories that you can use to enhance your arrangements. Look in magazines and books and on the Internet for ideas. If you're not good at arranging flowers, barter services with someone who is. For example, if you're a good cook, offer to trade baking for flower arranging.

76. Hang some of your children's artwork. Be creative. Buy some cork and cover the front of your refrigerator door to create a bulletin board for your art gallery.

77. Buy some ceiling fans. They're attractive, and they help cool your rooms in warm weather and disseminate the heat in winter, reducing your energy bills.

78. Make a new shower curtain from a sheet and buy pretty rings to hang it with. If you can't sew, have someone make it for you.

79. Save odd pieces of fabric. They can come in handy as the perfect contrasting ruffle on a pillow or as a new seat cover. If you're handy with a needle and thread, you can experiment yourself, or you can hire someone to do the sewing for you.

Projects to Avoid

No matter how much you try to rationalize, there are certain projects you should not take on when you've recently assumed a lot of debt. That doesn't mean you should never do them; you just should not now or in the very immediate future. Put these projects on the back burner.

80. Don't do expensive paint and wallpaper jobs unless you know you're going to stay put for at least five years. Ditto for window treatments and wall-to-wall carpeting that can't go with you if you move.
81. Don't tackle any remodeling jobs until you've lived in your house for at least one or two years. Until then you won't know what you can live with—or live without.
82. Don't finish your basement unless you know you or your children will definitely use it. The same is true of an attic.
83. Don't do expensive landscaping until you've lived through an entire year of different seasons and know what can survive in your climate. Then go to a local garden center and pick the brain of a salesperson about what works best in your climate and with the amount of sun and shade you have. You might also take a course on gardening at a community college.
84. Don't add expensive built-ins; you can't take them with you if you leave, and your tastes may change anyway.
85. If you hire someone to redo your driveway, do an asphalt drive with concrete sides rather than all asphalt or brick. It will cut down tremendously on cost.

86. If you have a slate roof and need to replace it, ask a roofer to use asphalt shingles that will cost much less than real slate.
87. There are copies of European original fixtures and chandeliers that cost thousands less than the real thing.
88. You don't have to have an expensive bedspread. A comforter is easier to manipulate and is less costly, and a dust ruffle and pillows will give you an expensive look for a very reasonable price. If you have to have a special comforter that matches your curtains, try to order something already made or hire someone to sew it for you.
89. You don't have to have everything your neighbors and relatives do; you probably never will have everything they have, so don't start trying to imitate them.

Projects to Dream About

You know about all the latest design and remodeling ideas, and you want to try them, but hold on. Your house was a big investment and you're only now beginning to build up your savings account again. Wait before you get more into debt. Dreaming is healthy. Prioritize the things you really want to do, and perhaps you'll be able to accomplish one big project each year.

90. Remodel your kitchen, including buying new cabinets and appliances.
91. Build deck, patio, or front porch.
92. Put in big, new whirlpool-style tub.
93. Install a walk-in shower.
94. Install an extra sink for a shared bathroom.
95. Build an extra bathroom.
96. Finish your basement and turn it into a media room or playroom.
97. Build another bedroom.

98. Finish your attic.
99. Create closet systems for every closet in the house.
100. Install an in-ground sprinkler system.
101. Build an at-home office with a door to keep people out while you're working and sufficient space for a computer, printer, fax, phone, papers, and books.
102. Buy a big screen TV and arrange comfortable seating so everyone can watch. Add some floor pillows for extra guests, plus a nice area rug for kids or teens to spread out on.
103. Build a laundry room and equip it with a washer and dryer, counters to fold laundry, and a sink.
104. Buy enough bookshelves for everyone's books and a file cabinet to store important papers and documents.
105. Install an electric fence so the family dog can safely play outdoors, or fence in your yard if that is allowed in your neighborhood.
106. Resurface your driveway.
107. Buy good-looking outdoor furniture that is functional for all weather. That way you won't have to drag it indoors when the weather turns cold.
108. Install new hardware on your doors.
109. Install new break-proof, energy-efficient tempered glass.
110. Build shelves in your garage for odds and ends and install racks on the garage walls for bicycles, ladders, and hoses.
111. Carpet your stairs.
112. Buy new area rugs.
113. Build a small greenhouse on the side of your house.
114. Install a swimming pool.
115. Build an outdoor hot tub.
116. Create an outdoor fountain or tiny pond.
117. Plant a wildflower garden.
118. Build a basketball, croquet, or badminton court in the backyard.

Preserving Your Investment for Now and for Future Sale

You may not think that you're ever going to move, but probably someday you will. It's wise, therefore, to preserve and enhance your investment by keeping your home well maintained while you live there. Then, when you must get the house ready for resale, you will face far less expense and manual work—and you're likely to get top dollar back on your biggest and most important investment. But exactly how do you help each room to put its best foot forward?

One of the first things you need to do is get your rooms spic-and-span clean. Scrub, scrub, and scrub some more so everything shines and sparkles. If you feel overwhelmed at the amount of cleaning you need to do, enlist your children and friends for a major clean-up session, and reward everybody afterward with a pizza dinner or a barbecue.

If the dirty handprints and other stains on your walls won't come off, you may need to repaint. You don't have to buy expensive paint; purchase reasonably priced paint in a nice cream color that appeals to a wide audience of buyers.

Clean windows, curtains, carpets, and furniture. Borrow a carpet cleaning machine from a friend if you don't own one. Replace shower curtains if necessary with plain vinyl liners that cost under $10. They typically smell very nice when they're new, like a brand-new car. Sew new pillowcases to cover old pillows. If curtains can't be cleaned, consider discarding them and leaving the windows bare, which is a nice contemporary look anyway.

Inspect your house from the outside. Look at the front door, shutters, mailbox, and lights, and clean all of them better than you ever have. Clean both the inside and outside of the porch-light cover to remove moths and their residue. Test the doorbell to see that it works. Be sure your house number is easy to see so people can find your home. If it's fall, rake your yard; if it's winter, plow the walk and driveway of all snow and ice; if it's spring or summer, be sure your flowers are blooming and your shrubs are pruned. Discard dead plants. Buy a welcoming doormat because lookers may linger at the front door.

If you live in a condominium, you also need to set the right clean mood in common areas. Go down to the lobby and remove all the pizza and cable installation flyers that have piled up or put them in a neat stack. Your neighbors will appreciate your efforts.

Houseplants, flowers, and shrubs that are in good condition say welcome, while those that are droopy say something negative about your housekeeping and maintenance habits. You don't have to buy fresh flowers, but you should display only healthy plants.

Your house should have a pleasant smell. If you're not sure whether it smells nice, have a friend come in and literally give it the smell test. This is particularly important if you have pets, whose odors you might fail to detect because you're so accustomed to them. Again, you don't have to buy fresh flowers, but you can use soaps or potpourri to give your house a nice fragrance.

Even if you love your possessions and collections, you should periodically eliminate clutter atop counters and bookshelves. Be sure that you can enter all rooms easily. You might need to do a bit of arranging, such as moving a chair or table, in order to clear a path.

Be sure that everything is in working order. Doors and drawers should open and close easily, lightbulbs should give the maximum amount of light, and your oven and range should work (check your pilot lights). Toilets should flush properly, caulking around bathtubs should seal completely, and blinds should be easy to operate. Incidentally, when prospective buyers visit, don't raise the blinds too high if you have an awful view; on the other hand, raise them all the way if the view is particularly lovely. And welcome your visitors with clean, fluffy towels and fresh soap in the bathrooms.

Most rooms have one sterling feature that you should play up for prospective buyers. Declutter the area around a fireplace that needs to take center stage; put only a few things on the mantel and don't place too much furniture around it. A nice hardwood floor should be visible rather than covered with wall-to-wall carpeting or a large area rug. Beautiful windows are only appreciated if they are not covered in layers of heavy curtains.

CHAPTER **6**

If It Ain't Broke, Check It Anyway
Home Repairs and Maintenance

Kenneth Austin, a home inspector in New Jersey, relishes telling prospective homebuyers an old joke about the value of a home inspection: "We like to think we help people buying a two-story house. One story before you buy the house and another story after you move in."

Before you buy your home, you should have it inspected to make sure everything is in working order, to find out the age of the home's systems and appliances, and to learn what needs to be tended to and maintained on an ongoing basis. You need to become a well-trained house detective, the Sherlock Holmes of homeowning.

Maintaining your home properly is much easier and cheaper than buying new appliances or systems every few years. If you don't paint the window frames every three years, deciding to wait ten years instead, the frames will rot and have to be replaced. If you don't clean the gutters, the rain will freeze on the roof in the winter and cause the roof to pull away from the house. And when the water melts, it will end up leaking into your home, possibly staining your kitchen floor or ruining that new paint job on your living room walls. If you don't mow your lawn, you'll have to endure the wrath of your neighbors.

A home is a living, breathing, and constantly changing environment. It is in a continuous state of deterioration, and if you don't maintain it, the deterioration will catch up to you and overwhelm you. A plumbing leak discolors walls and often gets worse. If water gets under your home's foundation, it can tip the building.

Systems such as central heating, central cooling, and interior wiring and plumbing need to be checked on a regular basis and maintained. Walls, ceilings, and floors, built-in kitchen appliances, insulation and ventilation, roofing, siding, and the foundation also need to be eyeballed periodically, preferably by an expert. It's not a bad idea to check for radon, termites, water damage, buried oil tanks, or lead-based paint, and pools, wells, and septic tanks should be inspected. It sounds overwhelming, and it can be. One expert estimates that there are more than 20,000 different components in any house. You are not expected to be an expert in all or even most of these areas, but at least you should have the resources to know what to do when trouble brews.

The Home Inspection

Before you even consider buying your home, find a reputable residential building inspector, and be there when the inspection takes place. It's a prime time to pick up maintenance tips, ask questions, and learn about potential problems. That way you can feel comfortable with the house rather than treating it as something alien. The home inspection is also an opportune time to learn the locations of the main cutoff valves for water and gas, the emergency switch for the furnace or boiler, the thermostat for the hot water heater, the main electrical switch, and the fuse box or circuit breaker box.

This house check has a two-sided benefit. Not only does it allow you to detect early on what needs to be upgraded in your home, but it also enables you to get to know your new home much like you would familiarize yourself with a new car and its idiosyncrasies.

A home inspection is not required by law so it's up to you to take the bull by the horns. Some lenders strongly recommend having one and will allow you to include inspection costs, which may range from $150 to $300, in the terms of your mortgage.

You find an inspector by asking friends and neighbors or by calling a homebuilder or real estate trade association in your area for a recommendation. Don't let the real estate agent recommend one for you because the inspector may be invested in helping that agent or company sell the home and may be a little less diligent in finding or citing problems. You want someone who is totally on your side. If problems are discovered before you buy the property, you can negotiate with the seller to foot the bill to remedy them or at least work out a plan for sharing the costs.

What's checked during an inspection? According to Fannie Mae's *A Guide to Successful Homeownership,* a thorough inspection will include investigation of the foundation; doors and windows; roof and siding; plumbing and electrical systems; heating and air-conditioning systems; ceiling, walls, and floors; insulation; ventilation; septic tanks; wells or sewer lines; and common areas in the case of a condo or cooperative apartment.

Luckily, many cures for what ails your home are simple, inexpensive, and avoidable if problems are caught early enough. So keep your home in good shape. It's your job to be the paramedic, ready to patch and fix at a moment's notice.

There are no inspection police knocking at your door to keep you on your toes about maintaining your home and checking it each year for problems. Put yourself on a home-check schedule and mark significant dates on your calendar. You go for an annual physical, a yearly car inspection, a biannual dental checkup. Give your new home a checkup too, at least once or twice a year. Time it to coincide with an event such as one of your children's birthdays or a holiday if that helps you remember to do it.

Of course, some things will need attention more often than once a year. How do you know what to check and when?

Planning for Home Improvements

Start by making lists of things that need improvement, repair, or replacement now or in the near future. Keep a notebook or tape recorder handy so you can readily record your ideas during the first weeks or months after you do your initial house check. Have your spouse do the same, then pool your ideas.

List things you like about your house and note what seems to be up to snuff. Record the age of your equipment—your washer, dryer, and dishwasher, for example—and check the list at the end of this book for the typical lifespan of these appliances.

Set aside a budget for must-do household repairs. You need hot water, you need a working oven and refrigerator, and you need heat, but perhaps you can do without your dishwasher for a while, and a clothes dryer is not essential if a public laundromat is down the street.

When you've decided which problems you'll need to tackle, plan how you will solve them. Is your roof leaking in the family room? Do you need to have your chimney cleaned? Is the fireplace flu stuck? Is the wiring outdated? Does your siding need painting? What is your game plan?

If you want to add onto your kitchen because you need more cabinet space or a pantry, think about how you want to do it. Do your homework to see if it's feasible and meets the setback requirements for your lot, if that's an issue. Jot down as many ideas as possible about what you'd like to do. What color do you want your kitchen cabinets to be? Do you want built-in bookcases? Do you need a new water heater? And don't forget that when you add onto your home, you will need more homeowners insurance and your property taxes may go up.

Decide what has to be fixed immediately and whether you can do the repairs yourself or whether you'll need to hire someone else to tackle them. If you're handy, it might be easy for you to fix a leaky sink or to replace the flush apparatus in a toilet. However, experts say that even handy homeowners shouldn't mess around with electricity. If you have faulty wiring or outlets that don't work get bids from three electricians. If your cousin is an electrician, so much the better, as long as he knows what he's doing. If you need a new hot water heater, call friends for names of plumbers, or look in the Yellow Pages. Friends and neighbors are among the best resources. Trade associations are another great source for names. Call each recommended plumber for an estimate. Don't ever tell them what you're willing to spend or share with them other companies' estimates. If you have time, it's wise to check track records with the better business bureau.

Ask the tradespeople you call about their experience and availability as well as about cost. Request names of current and recent customers and talk with the people who are referred to see what quality of work the tradesperson does. Finally, ask yourself if the person you plan to hire feels like the right choice. Only hire someone you like and trust.

When it comes to choosing materials to be installed, look through catalogs or go see a product sample. Know what you need and how much. Keep watching your budget.

What if some work is completed incorrectly? The tradesperson should make the correction for free. If fixing it is too time consuming, then have the tradesperson come back and redo the job at no extra charge to you. Situations like these are why it's important to have everything in writing. Always have some type of contract or written agreement regardless of the type of job and who you're dealing with. Keep all receipts and warranties.

Staying on Top of Repairs and Maintenance

To stay on top of repairs, maintenance, and warranties, file all warranties, owner's manuals, and other documents from the previous owner of your home. Keep records of your own repairs, routine maintenance, and home improvements. They'll also be useful when you sell your home because they'll show you've kept it in tip-top shape.

Don't be a homeowning ostrich. If you see a crack in the wall, don't just say, "Gee that's aggravating." Find the cause. If there's a stain on the wall, there's a reason. A small spot gets bigger; it doesn't go away. If the ceiling sags or the air-conditioning isn't right, something else may be wrong. If part of your house is cold in winter, you have a problem to solve. There could be a clog—perhaps one of the kids threw something into the duct work. If you see droppings in the house, you may have mice or worse. If you hear funny sounds in the attic, you may have squirrels. Get rid of them. If the heating system makes noise, find out why. It's a warning, much like having a temperature is a sign of an infection. Find out what's going on.

New Jersey home inspector Ken Austin tells a humorous story about a client's home he inspected ten years ago. He told the buyer to regrade around the house because water was gathering in and around the garage. One year later, the inspector got a call. The homeowner and his wife were beside themselves. "We're sacred," they said. "When we go to bed on a cold night, our closet doors open. We're frightened." At this point they were thinking they had ghosts. When Austin went back to the house, he discovered that the couple hadn't done the grading he suggested around the foundation. Water was getting in around the garage and freezing. The couple's bedroom was above the garage. As the water froze it shifted the weight of the house enough that it caused the closet doors to slide open. Finally, the couple did the regrading.

There are several tricks of the trade of running and maintaining a home that may save you time, money, and palpitations:

- Install triple-pane windows and other insulation to lock cold and hot air out. Be sure your attic is adequately ventilated.
- Make sure chimneys, fireplaces, and stoves are vented properly so gasses won't be released into your house. Check the roof flashing each year.
- Change filters regularly to get the maximum efficiency from your heating and cooling elements. Clean them in season.

- Caulk is the greatest friend of the homeowner. Caulking prevents leaks that can lead to floods.
- Wax appliances with ordinary car wax to keep them shiny.
- Don't put wet shoes in the dryer. The bouncing around may break the heating coils.
- Repair a refrigerator door seal or door liner. It can be done by following a few tips rather than calling in a pro.
- Control room temperature with a timed thermostat.

Mechanical systems keep your home running like a well-oiled machine. Know where main shut-off valves and switches are and the location of your fuse box or circuit breaker box. Every appliance comes with a warranty, which is a legally binding, written guarantee.

Maintenance pays off. If you maintain systems and appliances on a regular basis, you can increase their lifespan by 50 percent. Many major problems can be avoided with low-cost preventive maintenance. If you caulk windows, treat wood, spray for bugs, replace roof tiles, rechannel rain water away from the house, and clean the gutters, the big repairs may not be necessary. It's fairly easy to caulk windows, but replacing them is costly and requires professional intervention.

Invisible Dangers

Pay attention to invisible dangers: radon, carbon monoxide from blocked flues, electrical deficiencies, and lead paint on window frames, doors, and woodwork in some homes built before 1978. In October 1999, Andrew Cuomo, Housing and Urban Development (HUD) Secretary, awarded $56 million in grants to protect some 30,000 children and their families in 13 states from the health hazards of lead-based paint in privately-owned, low-income housing. For information on lead hazards and disclosure information in English and Spanish, call the toll-free phone line at 800-424-LEAD or check the Internet site at <www.hud. gov/lea>.

Make sure you have properly installed hot water heater relief valves. They are a $15 item, which if improperly installed can
flood your basement. Check your home for asbestos. Many homes
built between 1920 and 1960 contain asbestos in pipe coverings,
floor tiles, and roofing materials. Most asbestos is found in the
attic and basement, so do a thorough search of these areas. Make
sure your drinking water is safe. One way is to check with your
town hall to see if any complaints have been registered. Also,
check for underground oil tanks, which can corrode and leak.
For a free tip sheep, "Detecting and Deterring Invisible Dangers
in the Home," send a self-addressed stamped business-size en-
velope to: HouseMaster "Invisible Dangers Tip Sheet," 421 West
Union Avenue, Bound Brook, NJ 08805, or visit the Web site:
<www.Housemaster.com>.

Warranties

Warranties are the buyer's protection. Newer appliances
are often still under warranty. New homes often come with a
one-year warranty covering construction and materials. There
are also extended warranties, where a third-party warranty company ensures the structural integrity of the home for years two
through ten.

Of course, warranties don't generally cover problems that
are the result of misuse, improper operation, or normal wear
and tear.

Confusion often arises with warranties because they differ
in length and coverage. A new oven might be covered for a year,
a roof for 15 years. Some warranties cover insulation and some
do not. You need to read the small print. A window may be under warranty for breakage, but if it was installed improperly,
who's responsible for replacing it when it breaks—the window
manufacturer or the person who installed the window? One of
the biggest sources of irritation with warranties is proving who's
responsible for a problem. A leaky roof may be the result of

clogged gutters or improper installation. If you need to resolve a dispute over responsibility, bring in an objective third party to make a determination.

Another big problem with warranties is keeping track of them. File them alphabetically by type of product and put them in a safe place. You might compile a corresponding list of products and dates of warranty on your computer as a quick reference.

Financial Help for Making Repairs

If something breaks, first check your warranty file and your homeowners insurance coverage (see Chapter 1). If they don't cover the problem and repairs will be extensive, there may be nonprofit or government agencies that can assist you in paying. Check with your lender or real estate agent.

Your mortgage may have included a Community Home Improvement Mortgage Loan designated for home repairs. According to Fannie Mae's publication, *A Guide to Homeownership*, this is suggested by lenders for rehab purposes. The lender offers 95 percent of the cost of modest changes, and the amount of the mortgage is based on "the sales price plus rehab costs or appraised as completed value, whichever is lower." To obtain this loan, you must have been able to pony up cash equal to two mortgage payments. You must use only licensed contractors, the work is monitored, and the money is put in an escrow account from which the lender withdraws funds for the repairs.

You can also obtain a personal loan or a second mortgage to pay for repairs (see Chapter 4). Fannie Mae offers the HomeStyle second mortgage, from which you can borrow funds to repair, remodel, or enlarge your home. There are also FHA Title I Home Improvement loans, home equity loans (also addressed in Chapter 4), and rehabilitation escrow accounts where the lender holds funds for rehab in a special, interest-bearing account. Any time you borrow money, ferret out the lowest interest rate and determine how much time you will need to pay back the loan.

Common Maintenance Problems Homeowners Face

Plumbing Problems

Too many of us apply the squeaky wheel principle to home maintenance. If it's not squeaking, we leave it alone. One of the major systems we tend to ignore is the biggest area for potential problems in any home—plumbing. Plumbing lines run throughout the house and there's an opportunity for damage anywhere. Both supply lines coming in from the outside and drain lines can become blocked or clogged. Little leaks in sinks, bathtubs, and toilets can become big ones. A little leak should be fixed before it becomes a cascade that rivals Niagara Falls.

When you have a leak, you're paying big bucks for both the water and the heating of that water. A continuous leak can cause structural problems in your home: wood can decay and the bathtub can fall in. And moisture attracts bugs; carpenter ants and termites are drawn to any area of wood that's softened by water.

A major source of water leakage is around bathtubs and showers. If they have not been properly caulked and grouted, over time you'll have water damage. If water gets behind the tiles, it will rot the backer board holding the tiles in place.

In fact, caulking is the most prevalent deficiency in homes, especially older homes, but the problem is so easily solved. If caulking is mildewed or has gaps in it, it needs replacing, and you can do it yourself at a cost of only $3 a tube. Caulk around the outside of windows too to keep cold air out during the winter and warm air out during the summer. Caulking enables you to separate the elements, dry from wet and hot from cold.

Insulation

Proper insulation keeps your home temperature controlled and saves you money. Sixty years or so ago, insulation was not put in walls; if you own an older house you can't do much about it without ripping out the walls. However, most of the heat loss in a home is upward. So insulate your attic. When you install the insulation, make sure the paper moisture barrier is facing in the right direction, toward the warm side of the house. And maintain adequate ventilation so the attic won't become a greenhouse. Hot air gets trapped in an unventilated attic causing the sheeting below the roof to rot. Make sure there are louvers on both sides of the attic, and install inexpensive automatic vent fans. You cannot afford to have the bottom side of your roof rot.

The Electrical System

If yours is an older home, you may have power problems if you don't upgrade the electrical system. There may not be enough amps for a modern home with video games, hair dryers, and computers. Overloaded wiring, incorrectly wired outlets, and exposed connections can cause both shocks and fires.

A modern home requires at least 100 amps, but most homes that are more than 50 or 60 years old have 60 or fewer amps. This probably worked for an older couple who turned out the lights when they left a room and didn't have many electrical appliances. But a family with children cannot survive on low amps. Experts recommend 240-volt service and at least 100 amps, with a disconnect at the panel box.

If you have only 60 amps, increase the power to your house by adding a larger fuse box or circuit breaker box. If the fuse box is old, replace it with a circuit breaker box, which offers more protection. From the larger power box, run additional circuits throughout the house. The upgrade costs about $1,000.

Also, in an older home, you might encounter aluminum wiring. This inexpensive substitute for copper wiring was used in the '60s. Aluminum wiring is an adequate carrier of electricity, but the connection points like outlets, fuse boxes, and circuit breaker panels are a problem because copper and aluminum are incompatible. Bad connections can cause fires. For around $40 per outlet, you can have an electrician "pigtail," attaching copper connectors to aluminum wiring so that the connections are copper to copper.

Another electrical problem is insufficient outlets. When people use extension cords, circuits can become overloaded and cords can become frayed around carpeting. Overloaded circuits and frayed cords are a major cause of fires.

A warning: Again, amateurs should not play around with electricity. Some minor things you can do yourself, such as replacing an outlet, but even here you need to take great precautions. Handyman electrical work is generally unsafe.

Air-Conditioning

Air conditioners require annual maintenance and a cool head. Change filters and keep them clean. If you have central air-conditioning, wash the outdoor unit with a hose and make sure the condenser is free of debris. It is not necessary to cover the outdoor unit, because it is designed to be outdoors, but some feel better doing so.

Inspect the indoor filter monthly and change it if necessary. As a rule, it shouldn't go unchanged for more than three months. Filters cost between $2 and $15. The better ones catch finer particles. Do research on the type of filter you wish to purchase, or ask a hardware store expert for advice. Filters also are now available in the home center sections of grocery stores.

There are some common problems with central air-conditioning units. They get dirty, refrigerant must be refilled and can leak out, and the blower motor or compressor may fail after a number of years or repeated exposure to electrical storms. A technical expert must discover and repair these problems. Under no circumstances should you expose your air-conditioning line to damage of any sort. Don't hang clothes from it, for example. And be aware of the age of your air-conditioning equipment when you buy your house.

Window units require the same maintenance as a central unit, but they are a little more difficult to take care of because they are in the window and are often up high. If you can pull the unit out, take it to your driveway and wash it out. This will help preserve the unit. However, be careful not to get water in the motor.

Tools That Homeowners Need

Tools are the nuts and bolts of any home. But stocking your toolbox can be daunting, expensive, and confusing because of the sheer profusion of products. If you're about as handy as Tim Allen on the *Home Improvement* TV show, it's tough to sort out what the basics should be. According to one employee at a hardware store in suburban St. Louis, for $80 to $100 you can buy all the tools you'll need the most for your homeowner's tool emergency kit. You can find the tools at hardware stores or home depot centers, or you can flip through hardware catalogs.

Stock your toolbox with the following items:

❏ Duct tape
❏ File
❏ Flashlight
❏ Hammer
❏ Handsaw
❏ Level
❏ Phillips screwdriver
❏ Pliers
❏ Plungers (one for the bathrooms and one for the kitchen sink)
❏ Power drill and drill bits
❏ Putty knife
❏ Safety glasses or goggles
❏ Slip-joint pliers
❏ Slotted screwdriver
❏ Tape measure
❏ Utility gloves
❏ Wall scraper
❏ Wrench

You also may want to acquire the following outdoor tools:

❏ Clippers
❏ Compost bin

❑ Fertilizer spreader
❑ Garden hose (at least 35 feet long)
❑ Hand-held leaf blower
❑ Heavy-bristle, wide broom
❑ Hoes (gardening and stirrup)
❑ Knee pads
❑ Lawn mower
❑ Lopping shears
❑ Pitchfork
❑ Pruning shears
❑ Rakes (for leaves)
❑ Shovels (one for digging and one for snow removal)
❑ Spade and cultivator
❑ Watering cans
❑ Weed-eater or string trimmer
❑ Work gloves

Take care of your tools and they'll take care of you and your home. If you don't keep them tuned up, they'll rust, chip, and fall apart. It takes very little time to keep shovels, spades, trowels, hoes, saws, hammers, and screwdrivers clean and rust free. Store indoor tools in a tool box that you keep in the garage or basement, and keep some WD40 on hand to lubricate them. Wipe wet tools with a clean rag to prevent rust. When you've finished a day's work with outdoor tools, wipe off the dirt and moisture. Sharpen the tools every few months, grease hinges, and replace missing parts. The benefits are many—the tools will work better and faster and save you time and money. And tools do not become obsolete.

Garden tools need special care because they're exposed to water, which may cause rust, and dirt, which eventually may corrode the tools. Following a cold-weather tool-care regimen is simple and will keep you busy with your tools until spring. This regimen involves draining, cleaning, greasing, repairing, and sharpening. Power tools require the most care.

Cold-Weather Tool-Care Regimen

Power tools

❏ Remove lawn mower engine shroud and clean cooling fins.

❏ Scrape the underside of the mower with a steel brush or stick.

❏ Clean carburetor and fuel system.

❏ Replace spark plugs every season.

❏ De-carbon values and do value job (4-cycle).

❏ Change engine oil (4-cycle).

❏ Replace or clean filters.

❏ Inspect cylinder (2-cycles) and clean exhaust ports.

❏ Adjust, grease, and lubricate parts.

❏ Sharpen and balance blades.

❏ Add stabilizer to fuel or drain fuel from all power tools.

❏ Check ignition on all tools.

Nonpower tools

❏ Wash nonpower metal hand tools with soap and water, and rub motor or vegetable oil over wood handles and metal parts to prevent rust.

❏ Clean rusty tools with lighter fluid. Wipe with a rag or scouring pad.

❏ Sharpen shovels, spades, trowels, and hoes.

❏ Wipe garden tools, then plunge them into a sand and oil solution, then wipe them again.

❏ Lubricate axles on wheelbarrows with WD40. Replace blades or tape handles on good-quality tools that are worn out, rather than buy new tools.

Winter prep. It's time to bring your lawn mower to a halt and hang up your tools and lawn equipment. You need to follow a few easy steps before you are ready for winter. Read about new seeds, grasses, trees, and bushes to glean ideas for what you should plant come spring. Then, dig in and prepare flower beds and plant bulbs. Be sure to clean any nonpower tools you've used. Next, clean your lawn furniture with a mild abrasive to get it ready to be stored for winter. Some wood and aluminum furniture is designed to be left out year round. To house your lawn furniture, get your garage or shed in order. Take a tool and lawn equipment inventory and make a list of what you'll need for spring. Shop for new tools and lawn equipment. Winter is the best time to do so because many manufacturers offer price discounts and eliminate interest charges.

If you need to know more about how to use tools, consult videos and books from the public library or locate information on the Internet. Home centers give free courses all the time. To find materials to make repairs, look in catalogs, visit trade shows, or shop at your nearest home store, where the help is trained to be helpful. Know how much of each material you need, and don't go beyond your budget. Prices can vary a lot.

Minimum Outdoor Year-Round Repair/Maintenance Checklist

1. Roofs: gutters, etc., chimneys, plumbing vents, flues, ventilators, air-conditioning equipment, TV antenna, skylight

2. Foundations: basement, crawl space, garage

3. Windows and doors

4. Grounds and yard—lawn tool care—paved areas, wood structure decay

Change of seasons outdoor upkeep. Put together a seasonal inspection checklist and mark your calendar. Make clean-up a routine.

Seasonal Preventive Maintenance

You can set aside two weekends a year, one in the spring and one in the fall, and do a thorough preventive maintenance check.

First on the list of unglamorous jobs is to maintain your gutters. Gutters keep your house from rotting, your lawn from flooding, and your shrubs from becoming overwatered.

The time to begin maintaining gutters is autumn. Cleaning them is simple if you don't have a fear of heights. Don a pair of garden gloves, climb up, and scoop out the leaves and dirt. Then hose out the gutter to check the flow. Your gutters should be re-examined in the spring. In fact, you should examine and clean gutters every fall and spring to make sure the runoff is smooth. If it's not, you may wake up one morning after a torrential thunderstorm and find a pool in your basement. Failure to clean the gutters may also result in structural cracks.

Your lawn and other outdoor plants also require seasonal care. Prune and mulch roses in late October or November. Cut them back halfway to avoid winter freeze. You will pull mulch away from the rosebushes again in March. Hollies, azaleas, rhododendrons, evergreens, and other leafy plants should be sprayed with a wiltproofing solution to help them stay healthy and to prevent their leaves from freezing or falling off. Dig up summer flowers and put them up in a dry environment such as in your basement for the winter. You will replant them in the spring.

Plant new flower bulbs in the fall. When their flowers bloom in the spring, you will cut off the flower heads with scissors and fertilize the plants. If you have an irrigation system, drain it in the fall and have it blown out to keep it in working order. Prune trees after the sap has gone down in November or December. For a list of the tools you'll need for those days of digging in the dirt, see page 131.

Your lawn requires fertilizing, liming, and seeding. Watch out for bugs, moles, and gophers. Water your lawn and shrubs in times of dryness; they won't survive without water. Mulch gardens to keep moisture in. If you don't take care of the lawn, it affects your home's curbside appeal.

Energy-Saving Tips to Make Your Home Safer and More Comfortable

You can reduce costs and make your home safer and more comfortable if you learn some energy-saving tips. Home inspector Ken Austin suggests the following:

- Reduce the use of exhaust fans in the kitchen and bathrooms. Fans remove heated air.

- Avoid opening windows and doors except to remove humidity or odors.

- Shut the door and turn off the heat to a seldom used spare room.

- Fully insulate the room that contains your furnace and water heater.

- Put weatherstripping around doors.

- Caulk around windows and door cracks.

- Clean leaves and rust from compressor-condenser units.

- In unheated spaces, insulate hot water pipes to prevent heat loss and cold water pipes to prevent freezing.

- Keep attic vents open so outdoor air removes water vapor. Insulate ducts to reduce heat loss.

In areas with changeable climates, grass seed is usually planted in February, August, and November. Fertilizer (lawn food) is typically spread in September, October, and November. Some types are spread in February.

Fixing versus Replacing

Most everything in your house can be fixed up to a certain point. You can replace a motor or blower fan or solve a duct problem in your forced air heating system and still keep the system going. However, once the internal elements in the system, like the heat exchanger, are totally worn, you have to replace the whole system. The same is true of air-conditioning. When you get to the point where the compressor is shot, it's time to go into replacement mode. Roofs have a lifespan too. The more expensive the roof, the longer its life. A flat roof requires a lot of regular maintenance, and it usually needs replacing every five to ten years. A slate roof, on the other hand, can last 35 to 40 years.

Benefits of a Smoothly Running Home

Certain home repairs can bring tax benefits. A safer home may mean a reduction in your homeowners insurance. If you put vinyl siding on your house, your insurance premiums might decrease, and you will no longer need to paint the outside every few years.

Once you're organized, maintaining your home in pristine condition will become an easy-to-keep habit. All it takes is a few hours on a weekend to sharpen, grease, and clean tools and replace any deficient or missing parts. A well-maintained house makes every task more agreeable, and everyone wins. Everything will operate more efficiently and last longer.

Seasonal Preventive Maintenance Checklists

Spring Checklist

Grounds

☐ Check driveways and walks for cracks and deterioration.

☐ Check window wells, dry wells, and storm drains.

☐ Check wooden fences.

☐ Check retaining walls to see if they are cracking, bulging, or leaning.

☐ Check all landscaping.

☐ Trim all bushes and trees.

☐ Check all outbuildings, porches, and patios.

☐ Check for proper drainage.

Foundation

☐ Check during a rainstorm for proper drainage away from house and garage.

☐ Check for evidence of insect infestation.

☐ Check for settling, cracks.

Siding

☐ Check for finish or paint deterioration.

☐ Check caulking at joints.

☐ Check stucco for soundness.

Windows and Doors

☐ Check for damaged screens or broken glass.

☐ Clean and install screens.

Seasonal Preventive Maintenance Checklists

(continued)

❏ Check weatherstripping and caulking.

❏ Lubricate window channels.

❏ Check for rot

Roof

❏ Check for loose, damaged, or missing shingles or shakes.

❏ Check soffits for signs of moisture buildup.

❏ Check flashing for lifting or poor seal.

❏ Check television antenna for sturdiness.

❏ Clean out all gutters and leaders.

❏ Treat wood roofs, gutters, and siding with preservative.

❏ Remove mold from shingles or shakes.

Plumbing

❏ Repair all leaking faucets and valves.

❏ Check well and components.

❏ Check septic system for possible pumping.

❏ Check and close all exterior taps.

Chimney

❏ Check mortar joints.

❏ Check chimney and chimney cap for smoke or water leaks.

❏ Check general condition.

❏ Check cleanliness, and if necessary call a chimney sweep.

(continued)

Seasonal Preventive Maintenance Checklists
(continued)

Electrical System

❑ Check condition of incoming service wires and supports.

❑ Have all exterior plugs fitted with ground fault connectors.

❑ Check electrical power distribution for overloads.

❑ Check and mark all circuits.

❑ Test ground fault circuit interrupters.

❑ Check circuits for overfusing or test circuit breakers.

❑ Check all plugs and connectors.

Insect Infestation

❑ Treat for ants and other insects.

❑ Check for termites.

❑ Check for insect damage.

Porch and Patio

❑ Check wooden supports and windows.

❑ Seal patio at foundation.

❑ Check roof for leaks.

Room Interiors

❑ Check all painted and finished walls for condition.

❑ Check baseboards for finish or paint deterioration.

❑ Check rugs for wear and tear and floor for signs of settling.

❑ Check for defects in floors and walls.

❑ Check all stairs and railings.

Seasonal Preventive Maintenance Checklists
(continued)

❑ Check ceiling for leaks.

❑ Check all storm and prime windows.

❑ Check for signs of roof or flashing leaks on rafters and insulation.

❑ Check roof rafters for straightness.

❑ Check position and condition of insulation.

❑ Check ventilation openings for nests, blockage.

Heating and Cooling Systems

❑ Have cooling system checked by an expert.

❑ Inspect and install room air conditioners.

❑ Clean all elements of heating system.

❑ Check condition of hot water heater.

❑ Clean and secure humidifier.

❑ Test and start dehumidifier.

❑ Check flue pipe for corrosion and leaks.

❑ Check and lubricate attic fan.

Plumbing

❑ Check all faucets, drains, and traps.

❑ Caulk around tubs and shower pans.

❑ Check all piping for leaks.

❑ Check all toilet flush mechanisms.

❑ Clean all strainers and shower heads.

(continued)

Seasonal Preventive Maintenance Checklists

(continued)

Basement

- ❏ Check for cracks or breaks in walls.
- ❏ Check for leaks in walls and floors.
- ❏ Check for condensation on walls.
- ❏ Check for rotting sills and window frames.
- ❏ Check for sagging floor joints.
- ❏ Check crawl space ventilation, insulation, and vapor barriers.
- ❏ Test, clean, and lubricate sump pump.

Kitchen

- ❏ Check all appliances for noisy operation.
- ❏ Clean and change range fan filters.

Fall Checklist

Grounds

- ❏ Check window wells, dry wells, and storm drains.
- ❏ Seal driveway cracks.
- ❏ Check condition of wooden fences.
- ❏ Trim all trees.

Foundation

- ❏ Check during a rainstorm for proper drainage away from house and garage.
- ❏ Seal any cracks.

Seasonal Preventive Maintenance Checklists
(continued)

Siding

❏ Check for finish or paint deterioration.

❏ Caulk joints.

Windows and Doors

❏ Check for finish or paint deterioration.

❏ Remove and store screens and install storm windows.

❏ Check putty at windows.

Roof

❏ Check for loose, damaged, or missing shingles or shakes.

❏ Check soffits for signs of moisture buildup.

❏ Check condition of chimney.

❏ Check flashings for lifting or poor seal.

❏ Check all gutters and leaders.

Plumbing

❏ Drain exterior water lines and open taps (in cold areas).

❏ Insulate water lines that are susceptible to freezing.

Attic

❏ Check ventilation openings for nests, blockage.

❏ Check operation of vent and/or attic fan.

Heating and Cooling Systems

❏ Have heating system checked by an expert.

(continued)

Seasonal Preventive Maintenance Checklists
(continued)

❏ Remove (or winterize) room air conditioners.

❏ Clean all elements of cooling system.

❏ Check condition of hot water heater.

❏ Test and start humidifier.

❏ Clean and secure dehumidifier.

❏ Service all radiators and valves.

❏ Repair breaks in insulation.

❏ Check for air leaks, then caulk and weatherstrip.

❏ Lubricate all pumps, fans, and motors.

Alarms and Home Security System

❏ Test smoke and burglar alarms and carbon monoxide detectors.

❏ Replace alarm batteries.

Provided by <www.housemaster.com>.

Low-Cost Home Maintenance Projects That Can Save a Bundle

A stitch in time saves nine when it comes to thorough home maintenance.

What to Do	What It Prevents
Seal roof flashings	Roof leakage
Clean gutters	Improper roof drainage and basement leaks
Caulk exterior trim, windows, and doors	Water seepage and leaks
Replace missing roof shingles	Roof leakage
Install or extend downspouts or splash blocks	Basement leaks, flooding, and soil erosion
Apply deck preservative	Premature wood wear
Trim trees over roof near house	Damage to roof and siding
Regrout bathroom tile	Loosened tiles and water seepage
Clean or replace kitchen exhaust fan	Grease buildup that can cause a fire
Check for termite tubes and carpenter ants	Structural damage
Clean clothes-dryer vent	Fire caused by clogged vent
Vacuum air ducts	Allergic reactions triggered by dirt and mold buildup
Change furnace and air-conditioning filters	Reduced efficiency and need for premature replacement caused by clogged filters
Fill in low spots at foundation with soil	Basement leaks and flooding

Provided by <www.housemaster.com>.

Average Life Spans of Common Household Items

Garbage disposal	5–10 years
Trash compactor	7–12 years
Stove	15–25 years
Dishwasher	7–12 years
Refrigerator	10–18 years
Faucets	8–12 years
Toilet mechanism	5–10 years
Bathroom sink	10+ years
Washer	10–12 years
Dryer	10–15 years
Water heater	8–15 years
Plumbing	30–60 years
Central air unit	6–10 years
Septic system	20+ years
Paint	4–7 years
Stucco siding	40+ years
Asphalt shingle roof	15–18 years
Wood roof	15–20 years
Tile roof	40+ years

With minor care and maintenance, you can eke out the longest life from your appliances and systems. But everything has a life span. As a rule, once your home is about 20 years old, major items start to break down.

Provided by <www.HouseMaster.com> (Homeowner Information Center, 1999).

Five Important Things You Can Easily Forget about in Your Home

1. Change air filters on a regular basis. This can be done for about $1 a filter and can help you save on energy bills.

2. Divert rainwater from the house by installing down-spouts, elbows, and splash blocks. Cost: around $10.

3. Install a set-back thermometer that automatically adjusts the heating or cooling system for peak and nonpeak times. Have a heating company install it for less than $100, and you will save much more than that in the long run.

4. Check roof flashings annually. You can do it inexpensively yourself or hire a professional roofer.

5. Look for insect activity. Spray to eradicate pests. The cost is negligible when you consider the thousands of dollars of damage the creatures can do to your home. You can have your house sprayed two to four times a year, or you can prevent pests from entering your home in the first place by doing an outside power spray in the spring and the fall.

Provided by <www.HouseMaster.com> (Homeowner Information Center, 1999).

Resale Home Deficiencies and the High Cost of Repair

System	Suggested Repairs	Cost Estimates
Central air-conditioning	Replace system	$1,500–$2,000
	New compressor	$800–$1,200
Central heating	Water boiler	$2,000–$2,500
	Warm-air furnace	$1,500–$1,800
Attic insulation	Improve or add insulation	$800–$1,200
Signs of lower-level water seepage	Waterproofing	$3,500–$5,000
	Sump pit and pump	$600–$800
Roofing problems	New wood shingles	$3,000–$4,000
	New asphalt shingles	$1,500–$2,200
Electrical system problems	Add or improve service	$600–$1,200
Aluminum wiring	Upgrade connections	$20–$30 per outlet
Plumbing problems		
Mixed piping system	Replace sections	$300–$500
	Shower pan	$900–$1,600
	Water heater	$350–$500
Poor pressure	Replace piping system	$3,000–$4,000
Foundation problems	Major repair or rebuilding	$6,000–$10,000
	Underpinning or support	$3,000–$6,000

Based on a <www.housemaster.com> study of 1,000 "used" homes.

FOR FURTHER READING

Baldwin, Ben E. *The New Life Insurance Investment Advisor* (New York: McGraw-Hill, 1994).

Breuel, Brian H. *The Complete Idiot's Guide to Buying Insurance and Annuities* (New York: Alpha, 1996).

Buchholz, Barbara B., and Margaret Crane. *Successful Homebuilding and Remodeling: Real-Life Advice for Getting the House You Want Without the Roof (or Sky) Falling In* (Chicago: Dearborn, 1999).

Cumberbatch, Jane. *Pure Style* (New York: Stewart, Tabori & Chang, 1996).

Detweiler, Gerri. *The Ultimate Credit Handbook* (New York: Plume Books, 1997).

Eldred, Gary W. *The 106 Common Mistakes Homebuyers Make* (New York: John Wiley and Sons, 1998).

Fannie Mae. *A Guide to Homeownership* (Washington, D.C.: Fannie Mae, 1999).

Feinberg, Andrew. *Downsize Your Debt* (New York: Penguin Books, 1993).

Fisher, Sarah Young, and Susan Shelly. *The Complete Idiot's Guide to Personal Finance in Your 20s and 30s* (New York: Alpha Books, 1999).

Garner, Robert J., et al. *Ernst & Young's Personal Financial Planning Guide* (New York: John Wiley & Sons, 1999).

Garton-Good, Julie. *The Frugal Homeowner's Guide to Buying, Selling & Improving Your Home* (Chicago: Dearborn, 1999).

Glink, Ilyce R. *100 Questions You Should Ask about Your Personal Finances* (New York: Times Business, 1999).

Godin, Seth, and John Parmelee. *If You're Clueless about Financial Planning and Want to Know More* (Chicago: Dearborn, 1998).

Guild, Tricia. *Tricia Guild on Color* (New York: Rizzoli, 1995).

Hammond, Bob. *Repair Your Own Credit* (Franklin Lakes, New Jersey: Career Press, 1997).

Hannon, Kerry. *Suddenly Single* (New York: John Wiley and Sons, 1998).

Hufnagel, James A. *The Stanley Complete Step-By-Step Book of Home Repair and Improvement* (New York: Simon & Schuster, 1993).

Kent, Cassandra. *Household Hints & Tips* (London: DK Publishing, 1996).

Kirchner, Jill A. *Mary Emmerling's Quick Decorating* (New York: Clarkson Potter, 1997).

Lawrence, Judy. *The Budget Kit.* 2nd ed. (Chicago: Dearborn, 1997).

Levine, Leslie. *Will This Place Ever Feel Like Home?* (Chicago: Dearborn, 1998).

Lipman, Ira A. *How to Protect Yourself from Crime* (Pleasantville, New York: The Reader's Digest Association Inc., 1997).

Madden, Chris. *Chris Madden's Guide to Personalizing Your Home* (New York: Clarkson Potter, 1997).

Mintzer, Rich, with Kathi Mintzer. *The Everything Money Book* (New York: Adams Media Corp., 1999).

Parikh, Anoop, et al. *The Home Decorator's Bible* (New York: Crown, 1996).

Pinkham, Mary Ellen. *Mary Ellen's Complete Home Reference Book* (New York: Three Rivers Press, 1994).

Reader's Digest. *Reader's Digest New Complete Do-It-Yourself Manual* (Pleasantville, New York: The Reader's Digest Association Inc., 1991).

Rossbach, Sarah. *Feng Shui: The Chinese Art of Placement* (New York: Arkana, 1995).

Rubin, Harvey W. *Dictionary of Insurance Terms* (New York: Barron's, 1995).

Simpson, Jill Kirchner. *Mary Emmerling's Smart Decorating* (New York: Clarkson Potter, 1999).

Stoddard, Alexandra. *The Decoration of Houses* (New York: William Morrow and Co. Inc., 1999).

Too, Lillian. *Lillian Too's Basic Feng Shui* (South Australia: Oriental Publications, 1998).

Walker, David M. *Retirement Security* (New York: John Wiley & Sons, Inc., 1996).

Ward, Lauri. *Use What You Have Decorating* (New York: G.P. Putnam Sons, 1999).

Wydra, Nancilee. *Feng Shui: The Book of Cures* (Chicago: Contemporary Books, 1996).

I N D E X

A

A.M. Best Company, 9
AARP, 19, 49–50
Accidental death insurance, 86
Actual cash value policy, 4–5
Address, visibility of, 57, 116
Agent, insurance, 7–8
Aggressive growth stocks, 81
Air-conditioning, 120, 121, 130, 141, 146, 147, 148
Air ducts, 145
Air filters, 147
Alarm systems, 35–39, 144
American Association of Retired Persons, 19, 49–50
American Lighting Association, 33
American Red Cross, 41, 43–44
American Society of Appraisers, 12
Anger, 52–53
Answering machine, 29
Appliances, 86, 108, 110, 120, 125
Appraisal Institute, 19
Appraisers/appraisal value
insurance protection and, 9–10
personal possessions, 12

Appraisers Association of America, 12
Appurtenant structures, 3, 39
Artwork, 12
Asbestos, 126
Assets, 94
Associated Locksmiths, 34
Attic, 111, 113, 124, 126, 129, 136, 143, 148
Austin, Kenneth, 119, 124, 136

B

Bank fees, 86
Bankruptcy, 69, 89–91
Basement, 113, 126, 145
Bathroom(s), 102, 112, 142
cabinets, 101–2
plumbing problems, 128
sinks, 146
Bedrooms, 106
Better business bureau, 8
Birdhouses, 101
Block clubs, 56, 58–59
Block parties, 59–60